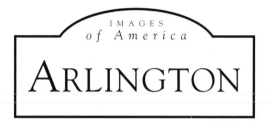

IMAGES
of America

ARLINGTON

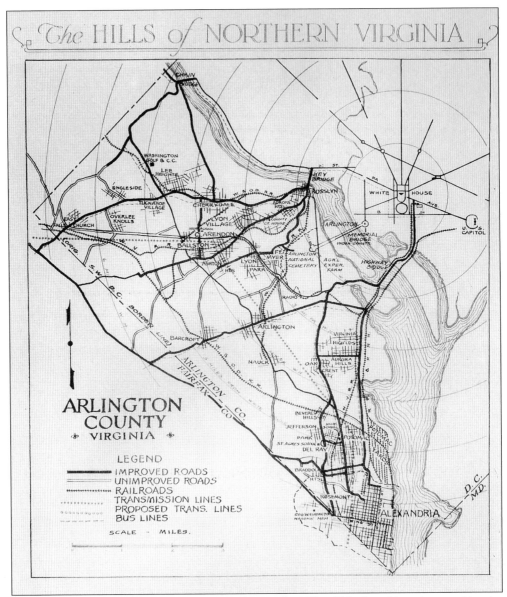

This map is copied from a promotional brochure, *The Hills of Northern Virginia*, issued by the Northern Virginia Bureau in 1926. It includes many of the communities portrayed in photographs and some (Del Ray, Rosemont, and Potomac, for example) that were annexed in 1929 by the city of Alexandria. As a result of that annexation and an earlier one, the Virginia General Assembly passed a bill forbidding annexation by a city of a county less than 30 square miles!

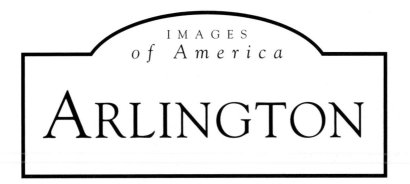

IMAGES
of America

ARLINGTON

Arlington Historical Society

ARCADIA

First printed 2000.
Reprinted 2001, 2003.

Published by Arcadia Publishing
an imprint of Tempus Publishing Inc.
Charleston SC, Chicago, Portsmouth NH, San Francisco

Printed in Great Britain.

Library of Congress Catalog Card Number: 00-106087

For all general information contact Arcadia Publishing at:
Telephone 843-853-2070
Fax 843-853-0044
E-Mail sales@arcadiapublishing.com
For customer service and orders:
Toll-Free 1-888-313-2665

Visit us on the internet at http://www.arcadiapublishing.com

At the end of each caption is a notation as to the source of the image. A list of the sources and their abbreviations follows.

Archives and Libraries:

AHS	Arlington Historical Society
ACPL	Arlington County Public Library
ACPL/DE	Debra Ernst photographs
ACPL/GS	Guy Starling photographs
ACPL/PD	Arlington County Photographic Documentary Project, 1979–1981; Paula Endo and Lloyd Wolfe, photographers
ACPR/WO	Arlington County Department of Parks, Recreation, and Community Resources; Fort C.F. Smith Park Historic Site Administrator Walton Owen
HOMC	Historian's Office, Fort Myer Military Community
McKinley	McKinley Elementary School Library, Arlington, Virginia
Styles	M. R. Styles Library, Falls Church, Virginia

Individual Donors and Lenders:

Baker	Gail Baker
Chaves	Tony Chaves
Daniel	Dorothy Robson Daniel
Drew	Mrs. Joseph Drew
Knull	Virginia Knull
Lane	Anna Belle Lane
McAtee	Robert B. McAtee
Saulmon	Catherine Saulmon
Syphax	Evelyn Reid Syphax

CONTENTS

ACKNOWLEDGMENTS

The Arlington Historical Society expresses its thanks and appreciation to the many picture donors and lenders who made this volume of Arlington history possible. First, we extend thanks to the archives and libraries: the society's archivist, James Palmer, assisted by Joanne Palmer, who spent many hours identifying and reproducing most of the photographs and other images for this book; the Arlington County Public Library Virginiana Room and Librarians Ingrid Kauffman, Judith Knudsen, and especially Jennifer King, who spent many hours finding and reproducing photographs; the M.R. Styles Library of Falls Church, VA, and Librarian Janet Daigle-Walden; the McKinley Elementary School library and Librarian Barbara L. Olivere; Fort C.F. Smith Park and Historic Site Administrator Walton Owen; and the Historian's Office, Fort Myer, VA, Military Community, and Historian Kim Holien.

The individual donors and lenders were Gail Baker, Tony Chaves, Dorothy Robson Daniel, Mrs. Joseph Drew, Paula Endo, Debra Ernst, Virginia Knull, Anna Belle Lane, Robert B. McAtee, Catherine Saulmon, the late Evelyn Reid Syphax, and Lloyd Wolfe.

No book such as this could be prepared successfully without its writers and editors, who came from the ranks of the society. Those who gave generously of their time and extensive knowledge of Arlington County's history were Gail Baker, Sara Collins, Jim Fearson, Jack Foster, Ingrid Kauffman, Allen Kitchens, Andrew Parker, Ruth Rose, Catherine Saulmon, Juanita Smoot, Karl VanNewkirk, and Willard Webb.

Special appreciation goes to Gail Baker for putting the captions and other written materials in final shape, to Sara Collins and Juanita Smoot for organizing the preparation of the captions, to Andrew Parker for writing the introduction, and to Ruth Rose for giving a final proofreading of the captions. The society also thanks Jane Casey for her assistance with artwork and Jim Murphy for his technical assistance to Jim Palmer in reproducing many of the images.

And finally, the society expresses its deepest appreciation to the committee that planned, researched, directed, and compiled this volume. Its members were Gail Baker, Sara Collins, Allen Kitchens, James Palmer, Andrew Parker, Catherine Saulmon, and Juanita Smoot.

This volume is dedicated to all who are represented in the photographs and other images. Their lives and experiences contributed significantly to the richness and diversity of Arlington County's history.

The primary sources for more information about Arlington's history and the people and places pictured in this book are the Virginia Room of the Arlington Central Library and *The Arlington Historical Magazine*, published annually since 1957 by the Arlington Historical Society.

Introduction

At the dawn of the 20th century, Arlington, then named Alexandria County, was about to enter its own second century. In the next 100 years, Arlington would change from a county of a few small villages separated by farms and pastures, to a bedroom community of the fast-growing nation's capital of the 1930s and '40s, to an ethnically diverse urban center. The photographs in this book trace the transformation in Arlington County through the 20th century: the early rural years, the development of the railroads and early suburbs, the 1920s, the influx of federal workers and their families during the New Deal and World War II, the evolution of the county to an urban community, and the redevelopment and ethnic diversification of the last 3 decades.

Arlington was formed out of Fairfax County in 1801 as Alexandria County of the new District of Columbia. This portion of the federal enclave west of the Potomac River was returned to Virginia in 1847 and continued to be known as Alexandria County until it was renamed Arlington County in 1920. During the Civil War, federal troops constructed many fortifications within the county and began burying their fallen comrades on the grounds of Arlington House (the G.W.P. Custis estate and Robert E. Lee's home), which they named Arlington National Cemetery. By the war's end, Arlington's Freedmen's Village had become the home to thousands of newly freed slaves.

By 1900, Arlington, which included some areas that are now within the city limits of Alexandria, had only 6,430 residents, many of whom lived and worked on the county's 379 farms. Scattered around the county were several small villages, including Cherrydale, Rosslyn, Barcroft, Nauck, Ballston, Queen City, and Glencarlyn, which were linked by unpaved country roads. During the first two decades of the 20th century, electric trolley lines and the Washington and Old Dominion Railroad were expanded into the Arlington countryside from Alexandria and Washington. These railways, like the Metro subway system more than 50 years later, brought enormous growth to the areas of the county that they served.

Growth continued during the Depression, as the expanding federal work force created a demand for housing. Arlington's farmland was filled with thousands of new homes as well as large apartment complexes such as Colonial Village, Buckingham, and Arlington Village.

During World War II, Washington, D.C., and its suburbs were flooded with military personnel and civilian workers supporting the war effort. Arlington's population doubled during the war, but the county began to become a place where large numbers of people worked, not merely a bedroom community. The Arlington Hall School was converted into an Army post, a Navy Annex was constructed on Columbia Pike, and most significantly, the Pentagon was built. More than 36,000 employees of the Department of Defense worked in that single building in Arlington County.

By 1950, the county's population had swelled to 135,000. This rapid growth brought with it a demand for more services. Many new churches, public libraries, and recreation centers were opened, and more than 20 new schools were constructed during the 1950s and '60s. Parkington, Shirlington, and other new shopping areas drew visitors to Arlington from throughout Northern Virginia.

Starting in the 1960s, some of Arlington's older commercial and industrial areas were redeveloped. In Rosslyn, bars, pawnshops, and car dealerships were replaced with high-rise apartments, office buildings, and hotels. The iron works and brickyards along Route 1 near National Airport became Crystal City, another urban neighborhood of multi-story buildings.

The completion of Arlington's portion of Metro in the late 1970s expanded this trend of urbanization to the areas near many of the stations. In the Ballston and Courtlands neighborhoods, storefronts and single-family homes built during the early decades of the century were replaced with high-rise structures. The Pentagon City Metro station, which initially was surrounded by open fields and a warehouse, became the location of a huge shopping mall, a luxury hotel, and office towers.

This urban development changed not only Arlington's physical landscape but also the composition of its population. What was once a racially segregated community became an integrated, multi-ethnic one. Beginning in the 1970s, increasing numbers of Arlington residents were persons who had immigrated to the United States from other parts of the world. Numerous stores and restaurants catering to these ethnic communities opened in the county. Other languages, particularly Spanish and Vietnamese, began to be heard in Arlington's workplaces, schools, and places of worship.

Since Arlington's creation, its history has been shaped by the federal government. Starting with the forts of the Civil War, federal construction projects have changed the county's landscape. In the late 19th century, Freedmen's Village, Arlington Cemetery, Fort Myer, and the Agriculture Department's Experimental Farm all had a significant effect on the county. Similarly, in the last 100 years, the Navy Department's radio towers, National Airport, the Pentagon, Fairlington, and the George Washington Memorial Parkway were federal projects that greatly changed Arlington's economy and character.

Beyond these construction projects, the proximity of the National Capital has indirectly shaped Arlington County in the 20th century. Early industries, such as farming, brickyards, and stone quarries, thrived in no small part due to the demand generated by federal expansion. The massive residential construction of the 1930s and '40s came about because of the need to house the tremendous numbers of new federal workers in the area. Finally, the increasing number of federal jobs that drew highly educated and well-paid professionals to Arlington from around the nation changed the politics and government of this once conservative, rural Virginia county.

While the tremendous impact of the federal government may have been unique to Arlington, a second force guiding Arlington's development also influenced growth in hundreds of other suburban communities throughout the country: transportation. In the horse-and-buggy Arlington of 1900, some of the county's larger population centers were those near two of the bridges across the Potomac: Rosslyn, at the end of the Aqueduct Bridge; and Jackson City, South Washington, and East Arlington at the Virginia end of Long Bridge.

As the electric trolleys and railroads expanded into the county, neighborhoods grew up near them, such as Glencarlyn, Bon Air, Clarendon, Ballston, Maywood, and Lyon Park. When the automobile became the predominant means of travel, parts of Arlington away from the rail lines began to be developed. The vast rural area north of Lee Highway began to be filled with single-family houses, and the Arlington Forest and Boulevard Manor neighborhoods grew up along Arlington Boulevard. Interstates 395 and 66 changed the landscape of the county and led to the development of more outlying areas of Northern Virginia in Fairfax, Prince William, and Loudoun Counties. The growth of these other communities affected Arlington by diversifying the region's economy. The most recent transportation advancement, the construction of Metro, brought the county's development full circle by reviving the areas along rail lines.

The photographs in *Images of Arlington* are primarily from the collections of the Arlington Historical Society, the Arlington County Public Library, and private individuals. The size of this book made the selection of images difficult and prevented telling the 20th-century story of every community in the county. We hope, however, that you will find this book both educational and entertaining.

One
THE CENTURY BEGINS:
1900

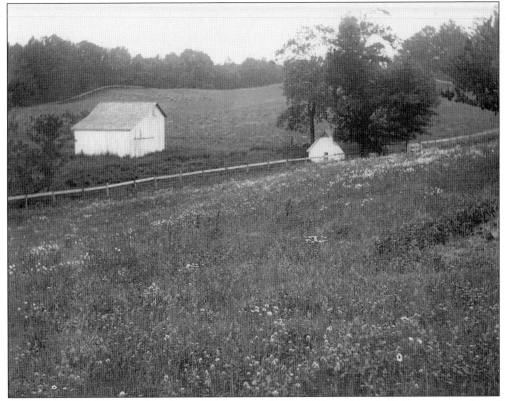

This 1903 photo shows a portion of Robert A. Phillips's farm, North Arlington, purchased following the Civil War. In 1866, Phillips planted 3 acres of Concord grapes, which flourished beyond expectations. So many visitors came to admire them that he suggested forming a Potomac Fruit Growers Association, with monthly meetings to discuss horticulture. The organization later expanded to include fruit consumers, who presented essays, musical compositions, and other cultural activities. It eventually became the Potomac Literacy Club. The mile-square farm on the Potomac Palisades, between Windy Run and Marcey Creek, was on what is now N. Quebec Street. (ACPL.)

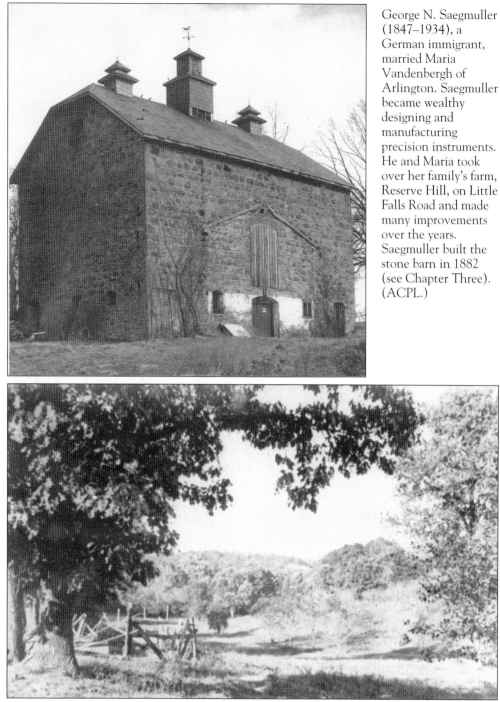

George N. Saegmuller (1847–1934), a German immigrant, married Maria Vandenbergh of Arlington. Saegmuller became wealthy designing and manufacturing precision instruments. He and Maria took over her family's farm, Reserve Hill, on Little Falls Road and made many improvements over the years. Saegmuller built the stone barn in 1882 (see Chapter Three). (ACPL.)

Harry A. Lockwood built a home on this tract shortly before the Civil War. The farm, shown in this c. 1895 photo and located along N. Glebe Road, was known as Easter Spring Farm. According to Eleanor Templeman, the farm was noted for its excellent berries, and schools closed when the berries ripened so that the children and their parents could pick them. They were paid 1.5¢ per quart for blackberries, 2¢ for strawberries, and 3¢ for raspberries. (AHS.)

This photo was taken about 1899 in present-day Clarendon at the intersection of Wilson Boulevard and N. Highland Street. The corn was being grown by William Ball. The boy, named Al Thomson, is on a horse that belonged to Ned Thomson, his father and a lieutenant in Lt. Col. John S. Mosby's rangers. The horse became famous because of his extreme age, dying at the age of 38. (ACPL.)

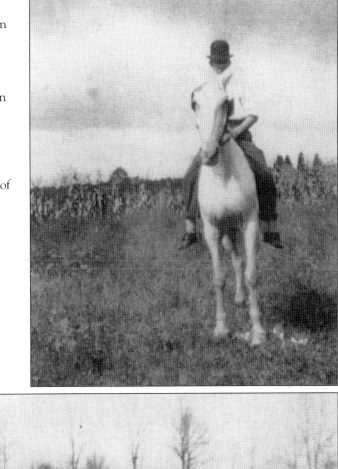

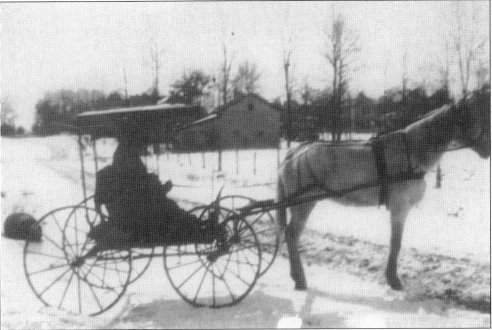

This picture was taken in 1911, looking east along Wilson Boulevard from N. Fillmore Street. The barn is a stable of George H. Rucker and is on the land now occupied by Fresh Fields. The horse and buggy belonged to Ned Thomson, who probably is the figure in the buggy. (ACPL.)

11

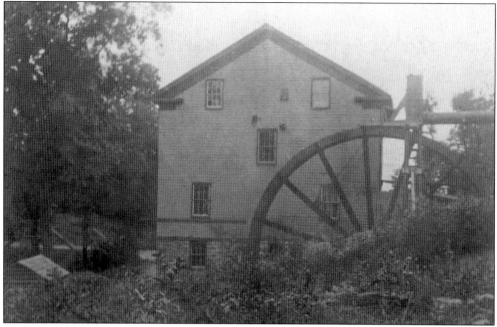

George Washington Parke Custis built a gristmill on Four Mile Run on Columbia Pike in 1836. In 1880, Dr. John Barcroft of New Jersey purchased the mill, rebuilding and renaming it Arlington Mill. Eventually, both the mill and the surrounding section of the county took the name Barcroft. (AHS.)

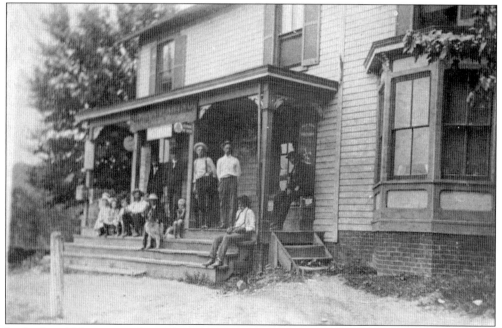

In this late 19th-century photo, the general store run by Oscar Haring and his family stood near the present intersection of Columbia Pike and S. Buchanan Street. By 1905, Barcroft included the Harings' store, the Arlington Mill, a railroad stop, a farm implement shop, and about 20 residences. The Barcroft Post Office was in the store. (AHS.)

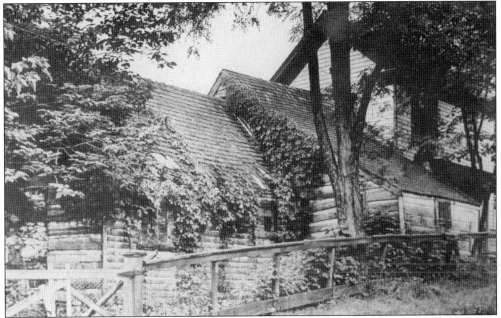

This 1908 photo shows the Old Mansion House, as it was known at the time in Glencarlyn. The left portion, torn down in 1915, contained the kitchen. The center section contains a two-room log cabin with a loft, built by John Ball in the 1740s. The two-story portion on the right dates from the late 19th century. The house, now known as the Ball-Sellers House, is probably the oldest building extant in Arlington. The Arlington Historical Society owns it. (AHS.)

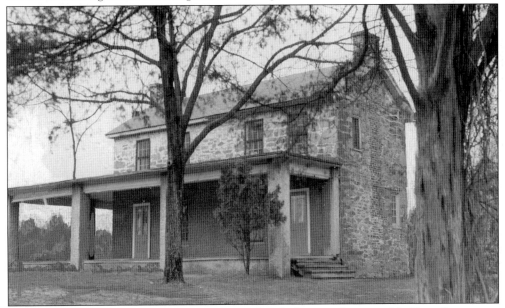

The Dawson-Bailey House, shown in this undated photograph, is on N. Troy Street near Twenty-first Street. The oldest portion, on the left, probably dates from the late 18th or early 19th century, when the area was owned by John Mason. In 1859, Thomas Dawson bought the house and enlarged it to its present dimensions. It now forms part of the Dawson Terrace Recreation Center. (AHS.)

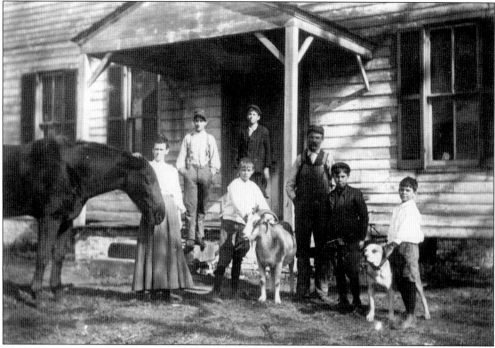

The Allwine family, shown in this 1912 photo, lived at Abingdon early in the century. This colonial house, built on the Potomac River, was once the home of John Parke Custis, Martha Washington's son. Our first president was a frequent visitor. The home was the birthplace of Eleanor (Nelly) Parke Custis, and she, her brother, George Washington Parke Custis, and other family members lived there. Abingdon burned in 1930 and the ruins are now located at National Airport. (AHS.)

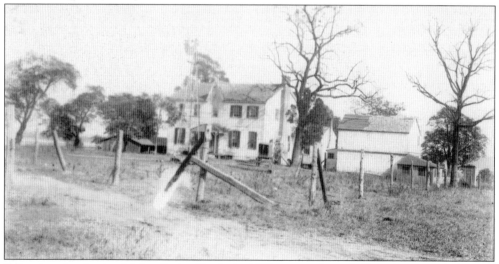

Following the death of John Parke Custis in 1781, ownership of Abingdon passed through multiple hands. By the early 20th century, when this picture was taken, the property was being mined for clay to make bricks, and some areas were leased for tenant farming. By 1930, preliminary restoration efforts were under way, but the house was destroyed by fire on March 5 of that year. (AHS.)

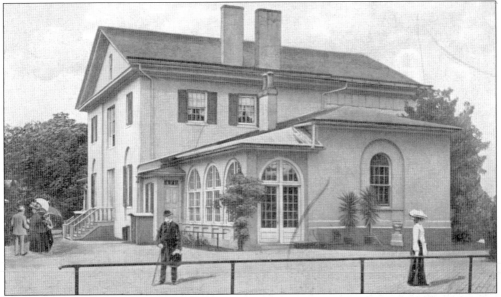

After the Civil War, Arlington House stood empty and neglected. Curious about the connection with Robert E. Lee, visitors to the cemetery often entered it. In March 1925, Representative Louis C. Cramton of Michigan introduced legislation to establish the mansion as a National Memorial with appropriations for the Army to restore the house to its original condition. In 1933, the mansion was transferred to the National Park Service to be furnished as a home with all original furnishings that could be obtained and antiques of the period of the years the Lees lived there. Today a third of the furnishings belonged to the Lees. For years it was known as the Custis-Lee Mansion. During the administration of President Gerald Ford, the name was officially changed to Arlington House, The Robert E. Lee Memorial. (Saulmon.)

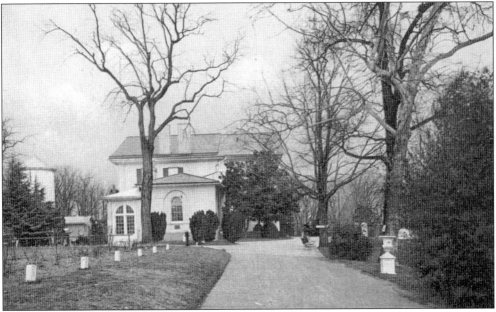

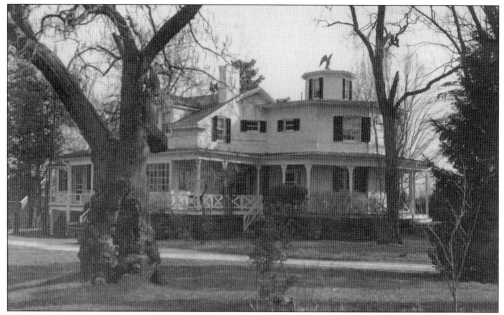

In 1820, a brick cottage (left portion of the house in this undated photo) was built atop the 1775 foundations of the Glebe House, a major Arlington landmark, located on N. Seventeenth Street near Glebe Road. The octagonal wing was probably added before the Civil War. The 1775 house was part of a "glebe," land supplied by the Church of England for a minister's residence and farm. (ACPL.)

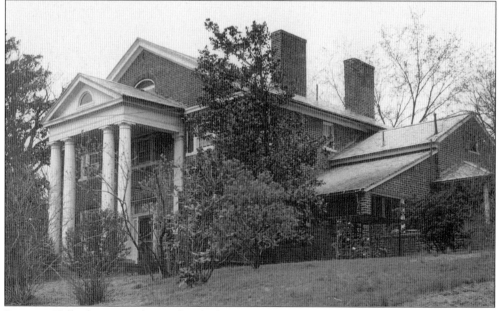

Prospect Hill, shown in this undated photo, was built in 1840-1841, on the north end of Arlington Ridge. James Roach, the builder, owned a gristmill and brick and masonry plants in nearby areas. Mrs. Philip Campbell purchased the house in 1913, restoring and renaming it Sunnyside. It was demolished and replaced in the 1960s by The Representative condominiums. (ACPL.)

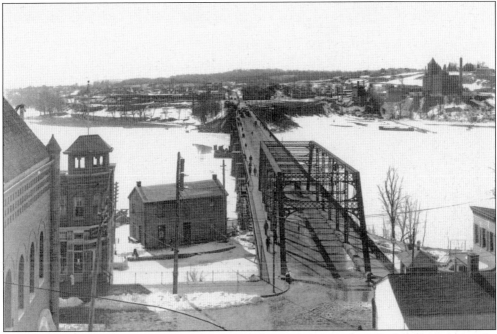

This view toward Rosslyn from Georgetown shows the Aqueduct Bridge, built over the Potomac in 1843 by the Alexandria Canal, Railroad and Bridge Co. to connect with a canal to Alexandria. The original Lock One in Alexandria has recently been restored. In 1923, the bridge was replaced by the Francis Scott Key Bridge. The building on the far right in Rosslyn, originally a brewery, became the Cherry Smash Bottling Co. during prohibition. Today it is the site of the Key Bridge Marriott Hotel. (ACPL.)

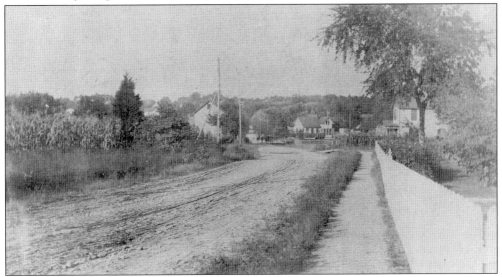

East Falls Church in the far western part of Arlington was a thriving commuter village by the 1890s due to early rail service. As typical of Arlington's complex boundary history, it was a part of Falls Church that fell into the bounds of Alexandria County and became legally separated from the town in 1936. Shown here is the railroad station southwest of the Lee Highway and Fairfax Drive intersection. (Styles.)

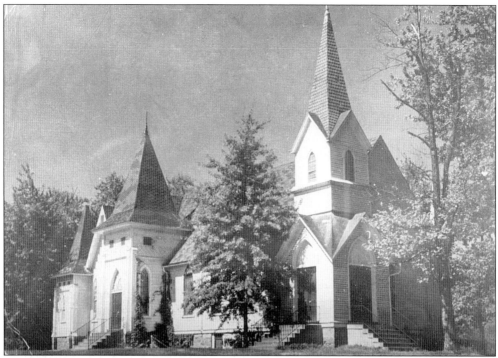

The First Presbyterian Church, Arlington, was founded in 1872. Between 1874 and 1876, the building shown in this undated photograph was built on the northwest corner of Wilson Boulevard and Glebe Road, where Peck Chevrolet now stands. It was organized as the Ballston Presbyterian Church in 1895. In 1951, the congregation moved to its current location at Carlin Springs Road and N. Vermont Street, and the church was renamed. (AHS.)

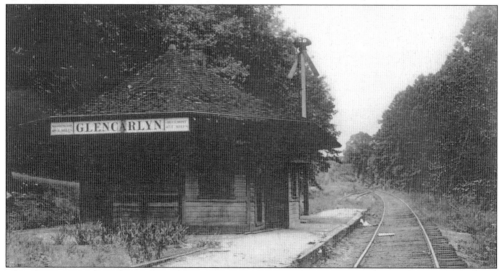

For a long time, the Glencarlyn railway station was a shed. The station pictured was built about 1890, and a telegraph operator was installed. Most of the residents worked in Washington. About 40 or so neighbors enjoyed a sociable time and became better acquainted as they waited in the mornings for the 8:00 train, which was often late. The station burned mysteriously one night just after a freight train passed. (ACPL.)

Monroe Grayson Chew, an early Glencarlyn resident, was an assistant superintendent of mails in Arlington. The village of Glencarlyn was developed in the late 1880s. Before that, the Carlin family had developed a resort, with picnic and excursion areas accessible by railroad, at the site of Glencarlyn Park. (ACPL.)

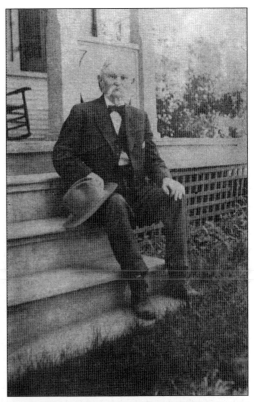

This is an unusual view of Green Valley Manor. Built around 1831, it was the home of William Fraser, who moved to Green Valley in the early part of the century. He and his family are buried on the grounds of Army-Navy Country Club, which occupies some of the Fraser estate. The house, which remained in the Fraser family, was destroyed by fire in 1924. (ACPL.)

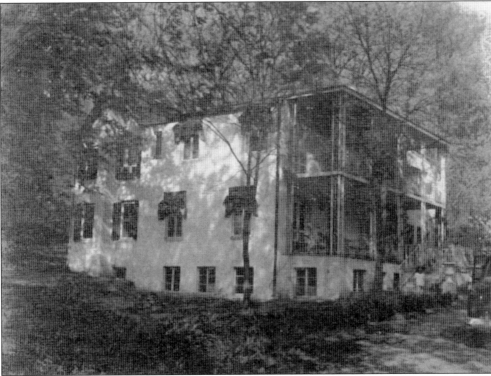

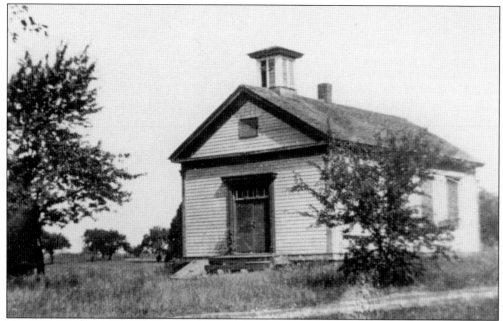

The Columbia Schoolhouse, shown here in 1890, was located on the north side of Columbia Pike at S. Wayne Street. The local (Arlington District) school board rented and later bought this private school and designated it No. 1 in that district. By 1899, plans were under way for a new school, and the building that opened five years later is pictured in Chapter Three. (AHS.)

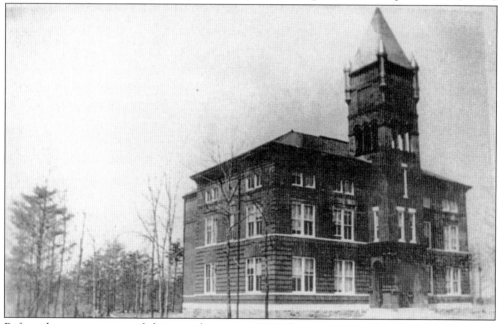

Before the construction of this courthouse in 1898, the county seat for Alexandria County (which included Arlington) was located in Alexandria City. The courthouse was built at Fort Myer Heights on Wilson Boulevard on the site of Civil War Fort Woodbury. A portion of this structure was incorporated into a new courthouse in 1961. The 1961 building was demolished in 1997, having been replaced. (ACPL.)

Two

ARLINGTON IN TRANSITION: 1900–1920

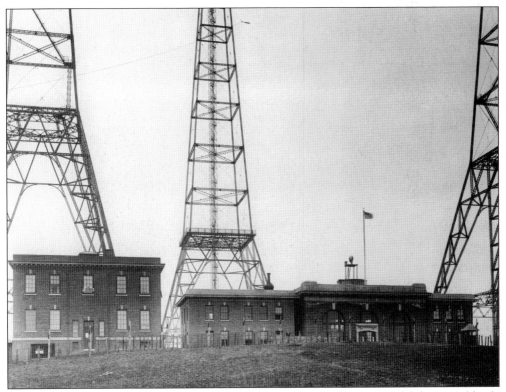

In 1913, the navy built Radio Station Arlington in an effort to establish a worldwide communication network. Pictured here are the three radio towers at Fort Myer. The use of the word "radio" to describe the new wireless communication was introduced here, as was transoceanic voice communication (in 1915 with a station broadcasting from Paris's Eiffel Tower). (AHS.)

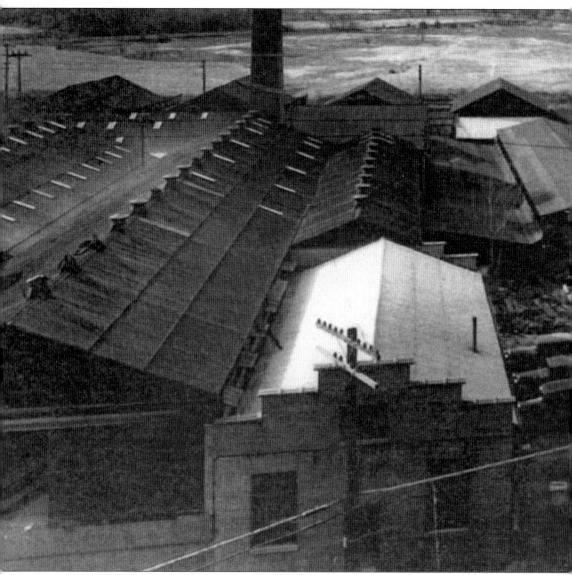

Next to farming, the manufacture of brick was the leading industry in Arlington County around 1900. There were several brick factories located along the Potomac River, including the WestBrothers Brick Company, shown here. Clay was obtained from the riverbanks. (ACPL.)

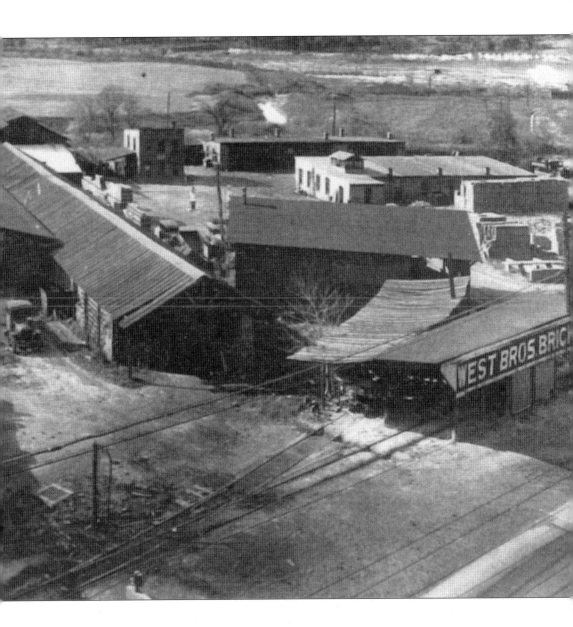

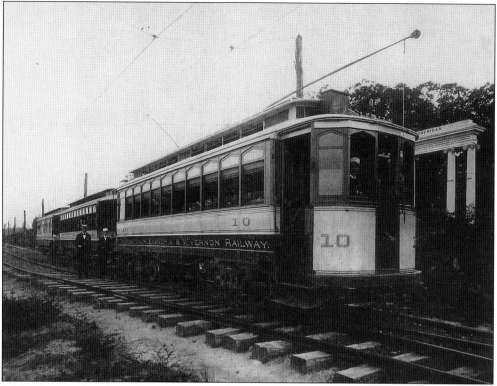

In 1896, the electric trolley came to Arlington. There was an inter-urban line between Washington and Alexandria and another between Rosslyn and Falls Church. In the photo, #10 stops at the Sheridan Gate of Arlington National Cemetery. (ACPL.)

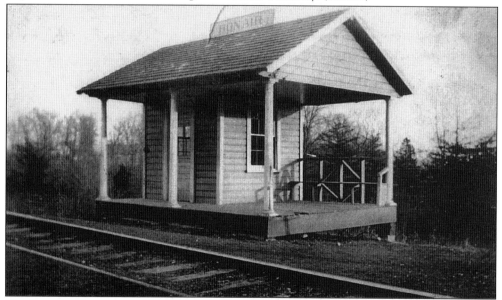

The Bon Air Station on the Washington and Old Dominion Railroad was on the Thrifton-Bluemont connector line, built about 1912. The station was located where Bon Air Avenue (now N. Kensington Street) crossed what is now I-66 and the W & OD Trail. (ACPL.)

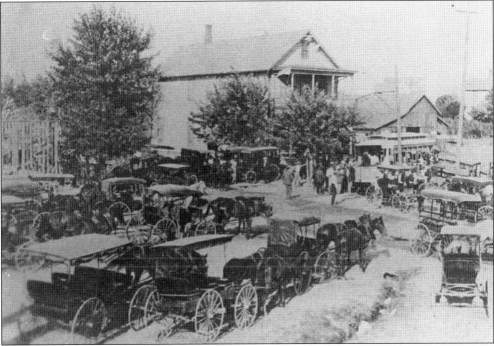

The railroad depot in East Falls Church is shown here in two photographs, the first taken about 1900 and the second (of the third station, built in 1895) in 1958. The depot was located near where I-66 today crosses under Lee Highway. Passenger service began through this area in 1859 on the Alexandria, Loudoun and Hampshire Railroad, which continued through a series of name and ownership changes, ending in 1951 as the Bluemont Division of the Washington and Old Dominion Railroad. Freight service continued for about another decade. (AHS.)

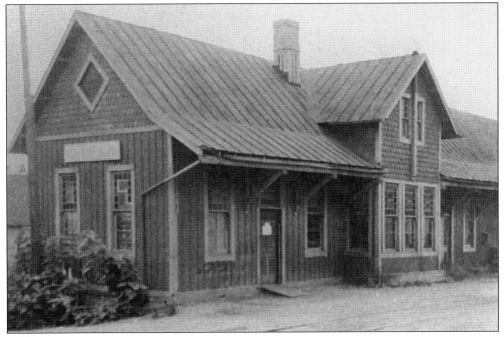

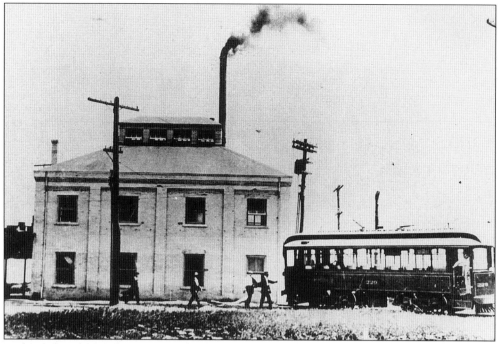

In the early 1900s, Arlington had two electric trolley lines, one running from Rosslyn to Fairfax and the other from Washington to Mount Vernon via the Fourteenth Street Bridge. In 1907, the two lines were joined near S. Eads Street and Army-Navy Drive. The station at that site, Arlington Junction, is shown here, c. 1915. (AHS.)

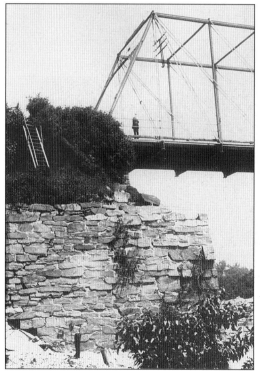

The name "Chain Bridge" comes from the bridge built in this location in 1810. That bridge was built with two chains made from wrought-iron bars that were suspended from massive stone towers and supported a wooden deck. There have been several bridges at this location. This photo, taken in 1915, shows the bridge built in 1874. (AHS.)

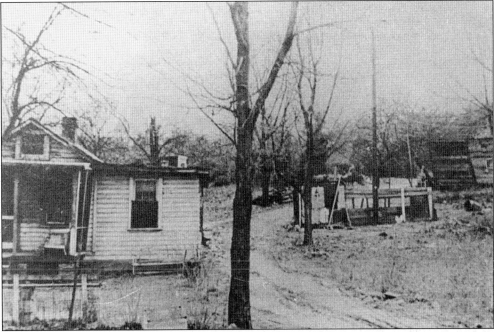

The Hall's Hill settlement shown here about 1905 got its start in the 1880s when Bazil Hall, a prominent Arlington landowner, sold 1-acre plots to some of his ex-slaves. *Polk's Washington Suburban Directory of 1927-28* listed Hall's Hill (unincorporated) as a town of about 300 people situated three miles from Washington. There was a post office known as Hall's Hill established in 1903 and discontinued in 1905. (AHS.)

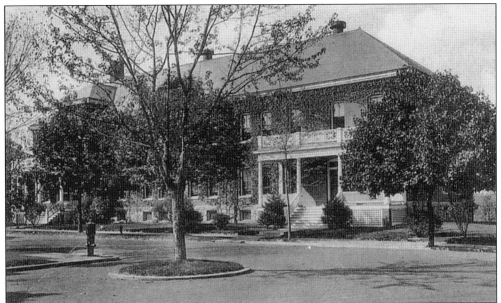

The military has had a long presence in Arlington. Fort Whipple, situated on the Arlington Heights overlooking Washington, was originally part of the network of defenses protecting Washington during the Civil War. In 1881, its name was changed to Fort Myer after Brig. Gen. Albert J. Myer, who had founded the Signal Corps here in 1869. (Daniel.)

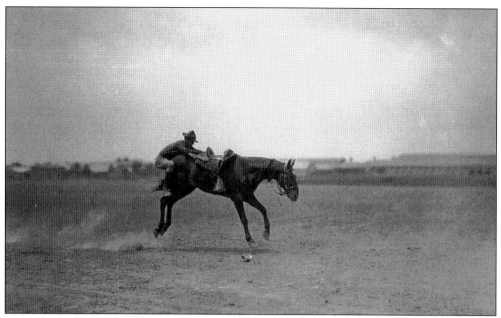

Fort Myer, originally established during the Civil War as Fort Whipple, became the Army's cavalry show post in 1887. A number of famous cavalry regiments were stationed there until 1942. This picture shows a member of Troop F, Third Cavalry, practicing his fancy riding skills. (HOMC.)

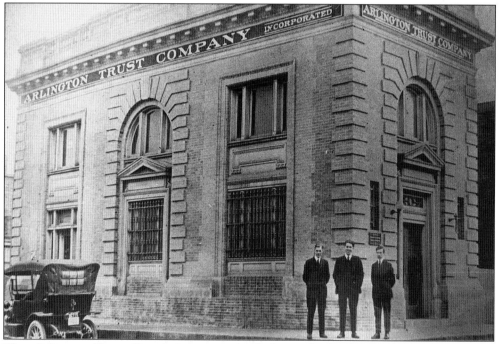

The Arlington Trust Company was one of the early banks in the county. Three bank employees—C.T. Merchant, Herman L. Bonney, and Bernard Boldin—posed for this 1914 photo outside the company's Rosslyn headquarters at Lee Highway and N. Moore Street. (AHS.)

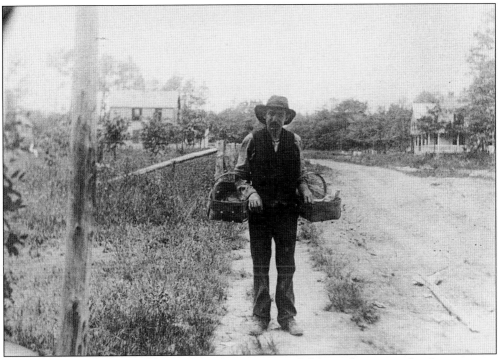

Tom Foley, an orphan, was taken in by the Harings and delivered groceries for their store on foot. This 1904 view is of present-day S. Buchanan Street in the Barcroft area. The building behind Mr. Foley, on his right, is a stable. (AHS.)

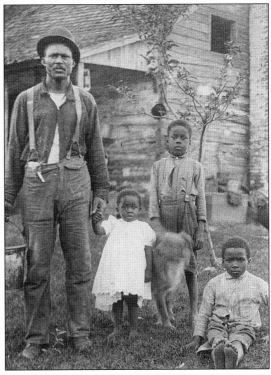

Moses Jackson and his family lived in the house shown in the background, c. 1916, probably Birchwood on N. Twenty-sixth Street, located near present-day Missionhurst and Marymount University. (AHS.)

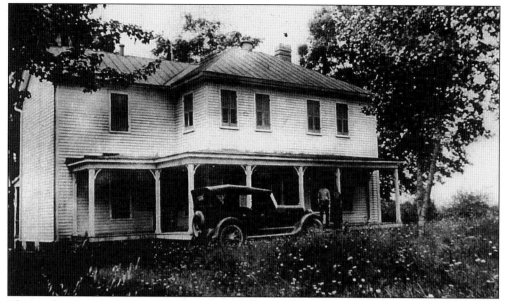

This is the 1913-18 home of Frederick and Leonie Claeys in Glencarlyn. Cars were rare in Arlington at that time, but they became common during the 1920s. By 1930, there were 12,008 vehicles registered in the county, or one for every 2.2 people. The roads were graded, except for a few that were maintained by the U.S. Department of Agriculture for experimental purposes. By 1930, 34 miles of county roads were paved. (ACPL.)

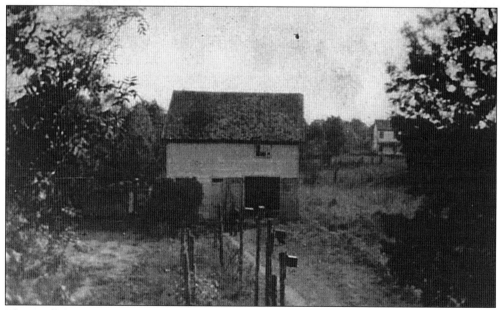

The small farm in Glencarlyn shown in this 1919 photo was typical in the county. In 1900, there had been 379 farms, most of them 3 to 10 acres. By 1924, according to a local directory, "truck farming prevails to some extent, but is rapidly diminishing due to the demand for land for home building." (ACPL.)

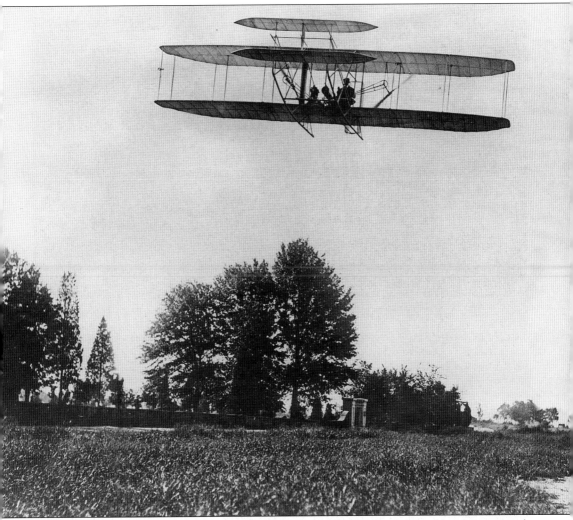

Fort Myer in Arlington was the scene of one of the earliest of Orville Wright's experimental airplane flights. This photo shows the "Wright Flyer" above the West Gate of Arlington National Cemetery on September 3, 1908. (AHS.)

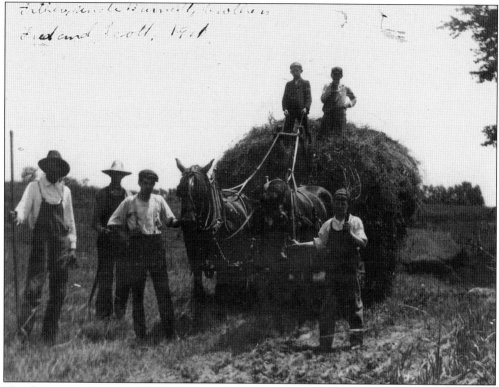

This hay wagon is pictured in 1911 on the farm on the Georgetown–Falls Church Road (Wilson Boulevard) that was operated by three generations of the Torreyson/Reeves family (1866–1955). Nelson Reeves, a Torreyson grandchild, shown here as a young man, was born in the farmhouse in August 1900. He went to grade school in Glencarlyn. The farm is also pictured in Chapters Three and Five. (Lane.)

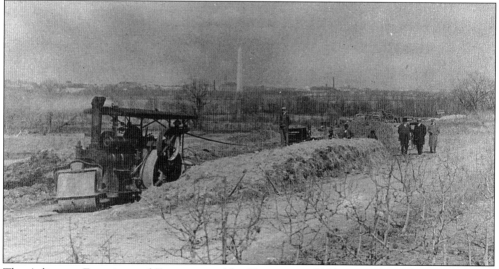

The Arlington Experimental Farm, created by Congress in 1899 to conduct plant testing, was operated by the U.S. Department of Agriculture until 1940 on part of the Custis-Lee estate. This 1904 photo shows Mr. Hull and his steamroller at the farm. (AHS.)

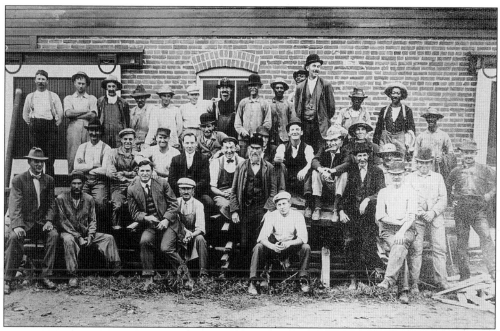

These were some of the workers at the Arlington Experimental Farm in 1910. (AHS.)

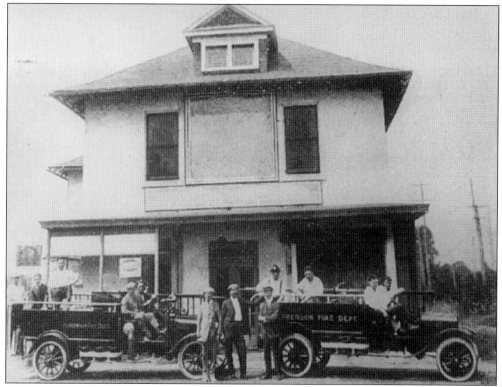

Until the 1930s, Arlington's citizens depended entirely on volunteer fire companies for their fire protection. The Clarendon Fire Department, formed in 1909 and shown here in 1920, was among the earliest. (AHS.)

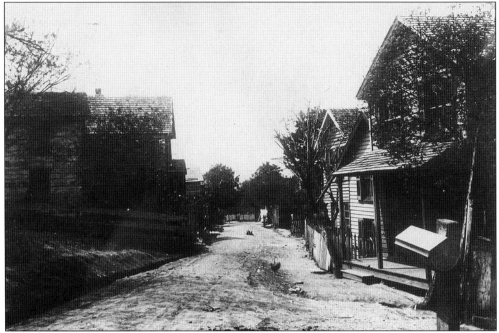

Queen City, also known as Mt. Olive Subdivision, was established around 1892 on land purchased by the Mt. Olive Church. Rev. Charles H. Vaney, who also ran a general store, started the church in Freedmen's Village. In 1910, there were 100 residents in the community. (AHS.)

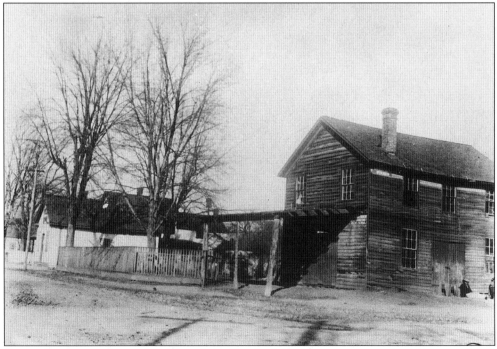

Queen City was condemned and demolished by the federal government in the 1940s in order to construct roads around the Pentagon. (AHS.)

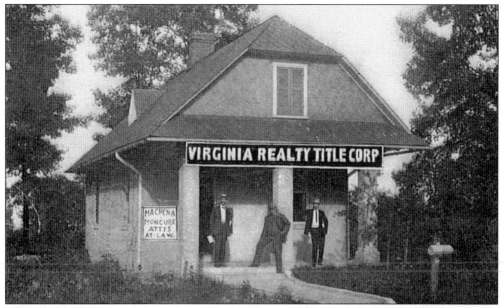

Virginia Realty Title Corp., constructed *c.* 1906 for Richard Cassius Lee Moncure, a judge, attorney, realtor, and editor of the *Falls Church Monitor*, may have been one of the first buildings constructed on Lawyers' Row across from the new courthouse, built in 1898. The building above was replaced in 1936 by a structure built for the firm of Adams, Radigan, and May. Lawyers' Row was demolished in 1990. (Baker.)

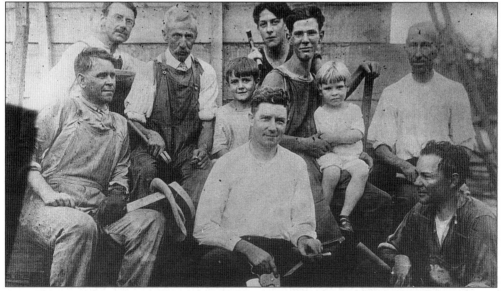

Neighborhood House was the first meeting place of the Rock Spring Congregational Church, located at 5010 Little Falls Road. The building was donated by Walker Chapel Methodist, disassembled, moved to its new location at the intersection of Little Falls and Rock Spring (then Jewell) Roads, and rebuilt on land donated by T.B. Jewell. Some of the church builders are shown in the 1912-13 photo. Pictured, from left to right, are the following: (back row) Mr. Dadmun, Clarence Hunter, three unknown people, Virginia Crocker Head, and Herman Smith; (front row) Howard Crocker, Lewis Buckman, and Nelson Jewett. (AHS.)

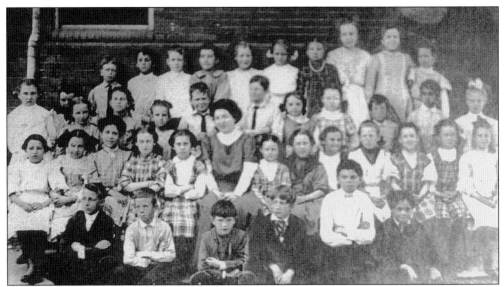

A 1904 photo shows the fourth grade class at Ballston Public School, built in 1893. After the Virginia Constitution of 1869 that mandated public schools was adopted, a village school was opened in the hall over Mortimer's (or Mortimore's) Blacksmith Shop. (AHS.)

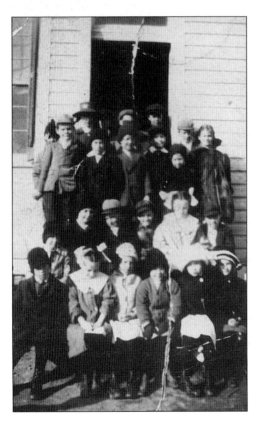

These schoolchildren attended the Saegmuller School in the northern-most part of the county in 1910-1911. The school, built in 1890, was named for George Nicholas Saegmuller, who advanced money for its construction. (AHS.)

Mrs. Walter Jones, shown in this 1918 photo, was a resident of Glencarlyn and an active member of St. John's Chapel there. Glencarlyn, first called Carlin Springs, was platted in 1888. (ACPL.)

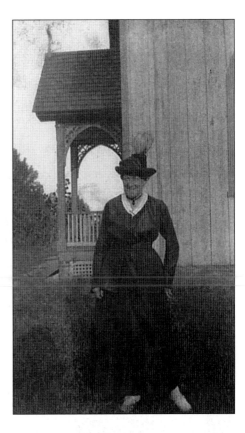

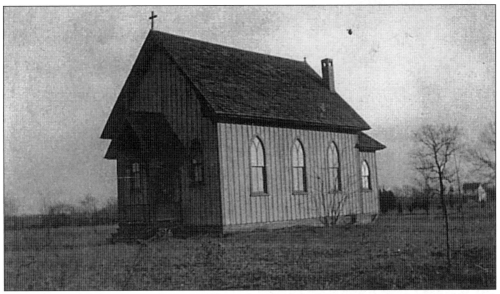

Located at 415 S. Lexington Street in Glencarlyn, St. John's Chapel was built in 1910 by A.J. Porter. The congregation began in 1890 as a mission church of the Virginia Theological Seminary and met in Carlin Hall until the chapel was built. The present brick church was dedicated on October 25, 1957. (ACPL.)

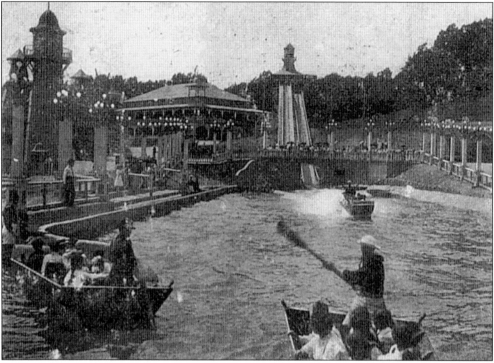

In 1906, Luna Park was built on 40 acres near the intersection of S. Glebe Road and Jefferson Davis Highway. Described by its promoters as "a fairyland of amusement overlooking the beautiful Potomac," it included rides, funhouses, a lagoon, a ballroom (shown in the next image), a restaurant, picnic grounds, concerts, and circus shows. (Chaves & AHS.)

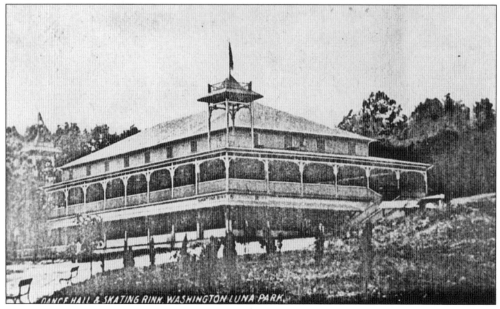

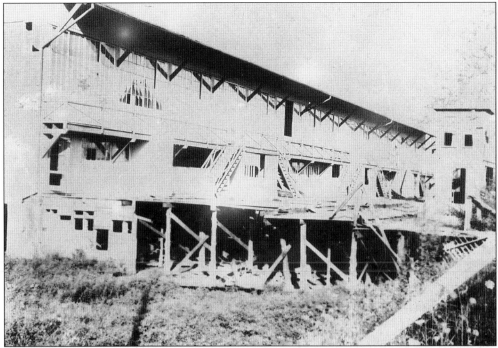

In the 1890s, two racetracks flourished in Alexandria County. One was located on Alexandria Island, near the entrance of the present-day Fourteenth Street Bridge. The other, called St. Asaph's, was in the Del Ray section of Alexandria. This is a photo of the grandstand at St. Asaph's. Commonwealth's Attorney Crandal Mackey closed down gambling after his election in 1903. (AHS.)

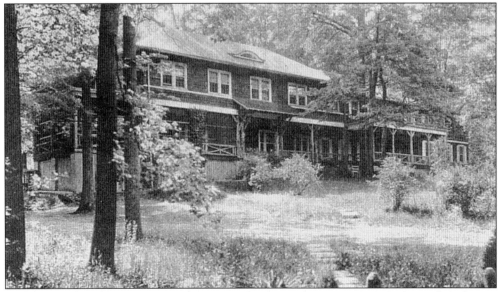

Vacation Lodge at the Young Women's Christian Association camp occupied one of the homes Dr. Joseph Taber Johnson built for his sons on his Lorcom Farm, established in 1907. The farm was named for these sons, Loren and Bascom. The lodge was replaced by Stratford Junior High School, but its memory lives on in the school's address—on Vacation Lane! (Daniel.)

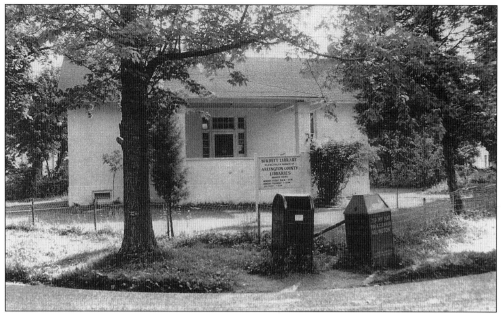

When Gen. Samuel S. Burdett, founder and leading citizen of Glencarlyn, died in 1914, he provided in his will for building a public library at a cost of not more than $3,000, with his personal library as a nucleus. The library opened in 1923. The Burdett Library joined the Arlington County library system in 1936. (ACPL.)

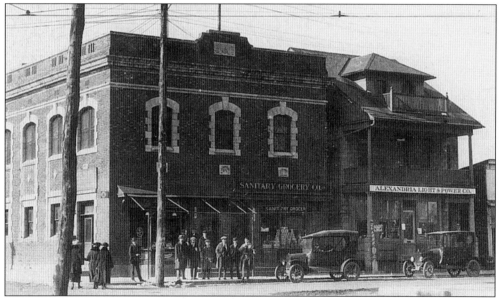

Columbia Lodge No. 285 of the Masons was built in 1909 on Wilson Boulevard in Clarendon. Depicted here in 1920, the lodge still occupies this building, which also has housed retail on the first floor, including Boyer's Pharmacy and Burkley's Bakery. Plans for the lodge were refused at first because "the county was too sparsely settled and it would be impossible for a lodge to exist in a pine forest." With the development of the adjacent communities of Lyon Park and Lyon Village in the 1920s, Clarendon became a major commercial area for all of Northern Virginia. (Daniel.)

Three

DEVELOPING A COMMUNITY IDENTITY: 1920–1933

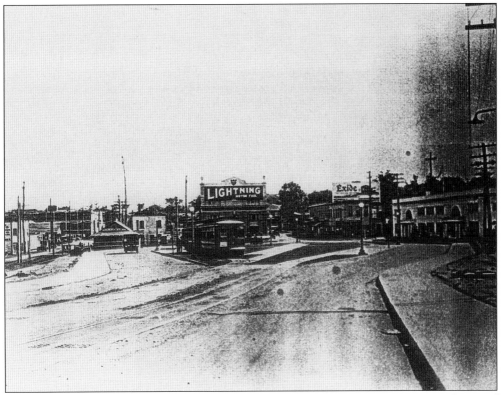

At the time of this 1925 photo, showing Rosslyn Circle, Rosslyn was an unincorporated town of 750 people. It was an important commercial and industrial center and the terminus of several rail and bus lines. (AHS.)

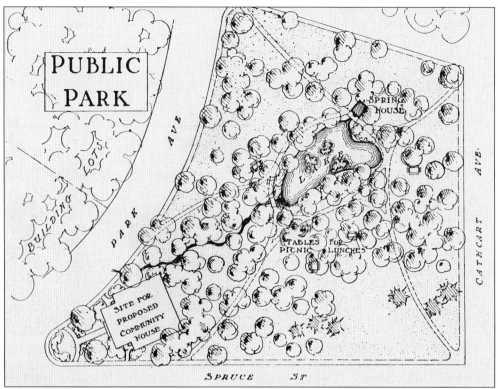

In a sales brochure for potential buyers, Lyon & Fitch described an anticipated 3-acre public park and a community house to be used for public gatherings. Early residents of Lyon Park formed a community association that initially met in the office of Lyon & Fitch. The company made a generous gift toward a fund for the construction of a community house, which was completed in 1925. (Saulmon.)

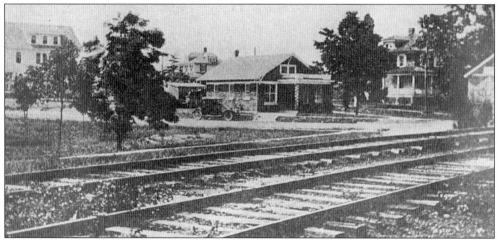

Rail lines were critical in Arlington's early 20th-century development. The office of developers Frank Lyon and Walton Fitch, shown in this 1925 photo, was across the street from the Washington-Virginia Electric Railway station, at the intersection of today's N. Seventh Street, Pershing Drive, and Washington Boulevard. Lyon and Fitch were the primary developers of Lyon Park and donated the land for the neighborhood's park and community center. (AHS.)

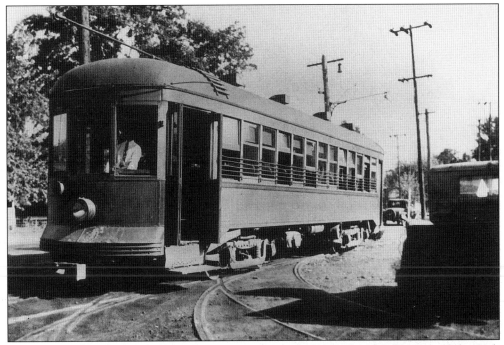

Rail lines were the major means of transportation in the county in the first part of the 20th century. By 1924, electric rail lines had 64 stops on the four branches of the Washington-Virginia Railway Company within the present county boundaries. The Washington and Old Dominion Railroad had 28 stops on the Great Falls and Bluemont Divisions, and an additional seven on the Bluemont Division into Alexandria. Automobiles replaced rail transport after World War II, and the last passenger train of the W & OD to Rosslyn ended in 1951. (AHS.)

The "new" Columbia School opened in 1904 on Columbia Pike, west of what is now Walter Reed Drive. It replaced Columbia Schoolhouse, a one-room frame building at Columbia Pike and S. Wayne Street (see Chapter One). After Patrick Henry Elementary was built as a replacement in 1924, this building housed the Columbia Pike Branch Library until it was torn down in 1941. (AHS.)

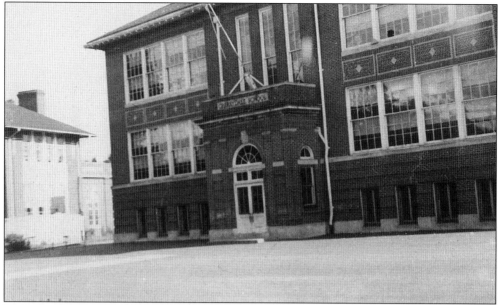

The Cherrydale School was built on Lee Highway in 1917 when an earlier 1907 building was found inadequate. An auditorium was added, and the school served as a gathering place for neighborhood events. The entryway to this new building was changed several times, and the school was closed in 1969 and torn down in 1973. A nursing home was built on the site. (AHS.)

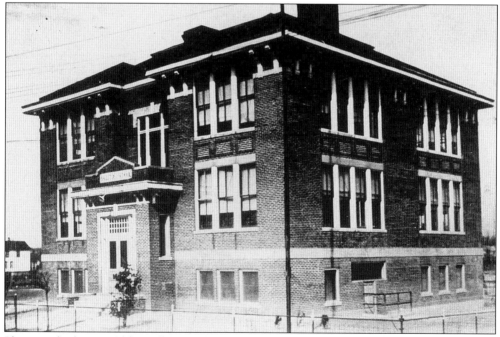

Photographed in 1930, the Ballston Elementary School was built in 1893 on Wilson Boulevard at Randolph Street and had the same floor plan as the Hume School. It replaced an earlier frame Walker School. William Ball (see next page) did carpentry work inside this new building. The brick building shown later became a Hogate's Restaurant. (AHS.)

44

The William Ball family home stood on Washington Boulevard near Clarendon at the current site of the American Legion Hall. Mr. and Mrs. Ball are sitting in chairs at the right end of the porch with their six children. Their son Frank (about age 10), sitting in front of them, became a prominent lawyer and politician. (ACPL.)

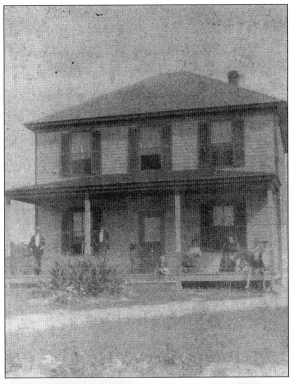

The Cadet Corps at Washington-Lee High School was in its second year as a Junior ROTC unit when this photo was taken in 1932. Shown, from left to right, are Tazwell Watson, John Green, Curtis MacDonald, Frank Myers, Solomon Iskow, Lt. Col. C.S. McNeill, Elmer Wiseman, Kenneth Byrnes, Warrant Officer L.S. Yassel, Warren Dodd, Robert McAtee, Robert Rollings, Harper Graves, Russell Springer, and Elmo Legg. (McAtee.)

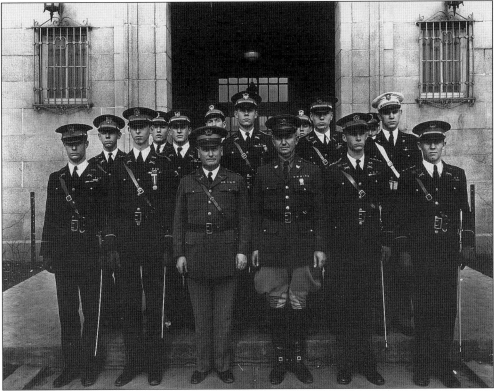

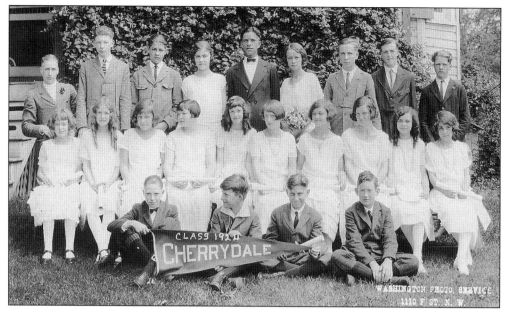

These students graduating in the Cherrydale School class of 1924 were photographed at the home of Wilbur Tignor, across the street from the school. Among those identified, from left to right, are (front row) Alice McAtee and Helen Patterson (second and third from right), a Miss Walton (fifth from right); the seated boys include Cleveland Topley, John Bell, and Kenneth Barker; and the standing boys are Edward Cahill, Bruce Hice, Walter Spates, Krug McCoskty, John Spence, and two unknown boys. (AHS.)

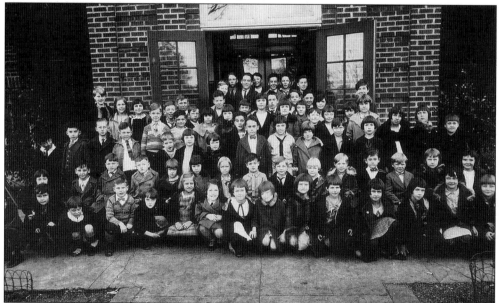

In a 1926 photo, students and teachers posed in front of the "new" Cherrydale School, built in 1917. The auditorium of the school was used as a meeting place for the community, which actively supported the school through the Patrons League. Many special events such as dinners, movies, dances, and pageants were held, and hot lunches were provided for the students. (ACPL.)

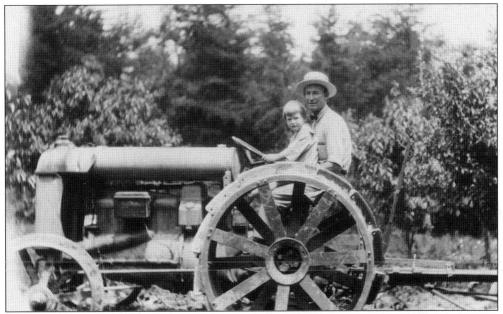

Nelson Reeves, shown here in 1927 with his niece, Mary Elizabeth Lane, was one of the last dairy farmers in Arlington. He also served his county 46 years as an election official and judge. After Arlington Boulevard (Route 50) cut through the farm in the early 1930s, a tunnel under the highway allowed cattle to get to the pasture near where Kenmore Middle School was later built. (Lane.)

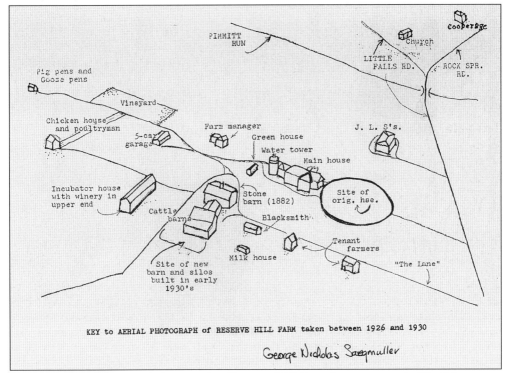

This is the key to the aerial photograph of Reserve Hill Farm (see next page). (Knull.)

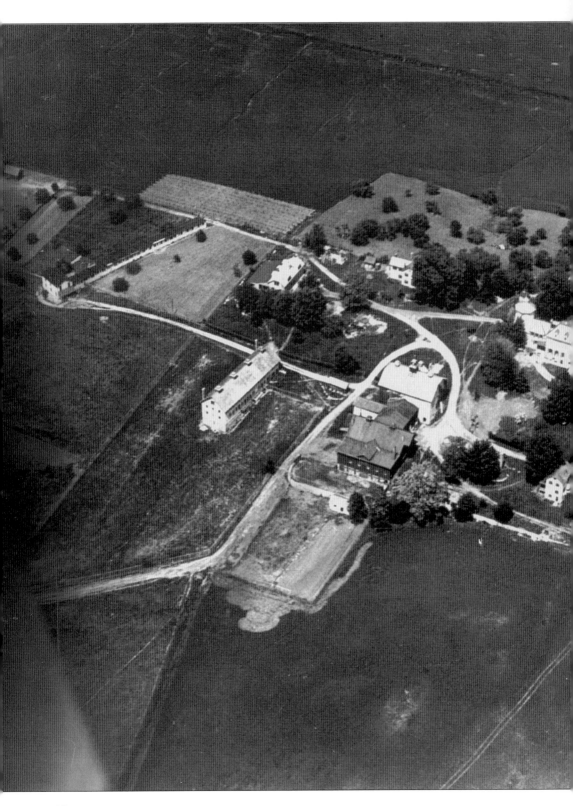

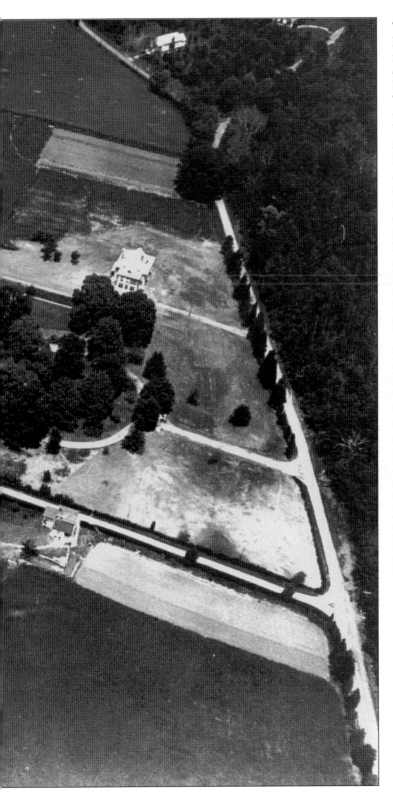

This aerial view of Reserve Hill Farm in the northern part of the county was taken between 1926 and 1930. The original house here was built by Gilbert Vandenbergh in 1855 and named Reserve Hill because of the Union Army Reserve units stationed nearby during the Civil War. His daughter, Maria Jane, married George Nicholas Saegmuller, and they continued to live at the homestead and added many improvements. After fire destroyed the house in 1892, Saegmuller replaced it with a home reminiscent of his native Nürnberg and added a stone water tower. He was active in county affairs and served as chairman of the board of supervisors. Saegmuller Public School, constructed in 1890, was named for its benefactor; James Madison School replaced it in 1937. The house on Little Falls Road is owned by the Knights of Columbus. (Knull.)

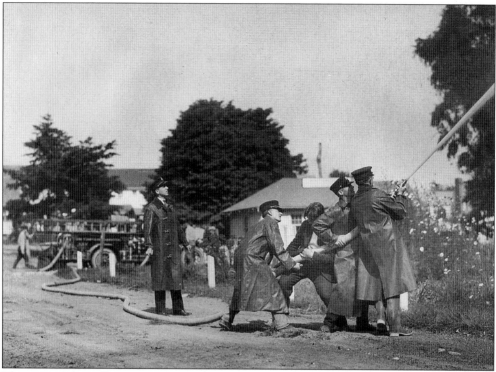

The men of the Jefferson District Volunteer Fire Department in 1925 at a practice drill with equipment include W. Glen Bixler, Frank Allwine, E.C. Rayle, and Frank Tracey. Once housed on S. Twenty-third Street, this department is now located in the Aurora Hills Center with a branch of the public library, a recreation center, and a visitors center. (AHS.)

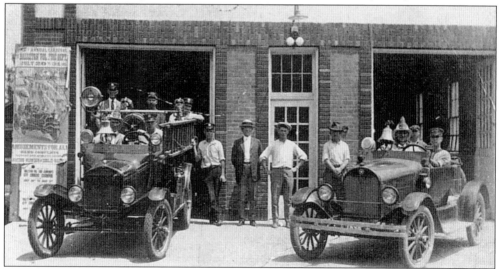

This postcard shows the Ballston Volunteer Fire Department, Company #2, in 1923. The company was organized in 1908, and its firehouse was located on Ballston Avenue (now Stuart Street) off Fairfax Drive. It may have been the first to use motorized equipment when it got a 1914 Model T Ford truck to carry soda acid tanks. (Daniel, with permission from Charles Satterfield.)

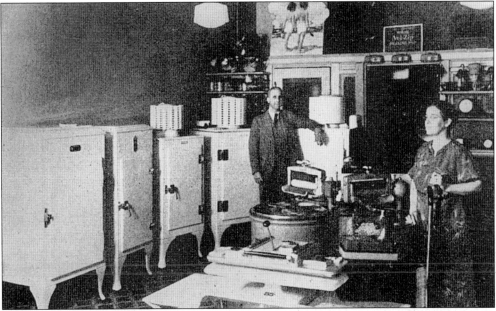

I.C. Warner, owner of Warner & Gray's Store, is pictured inside his shop in 1933 with a line of new refrigerators, while manager Eula T. Maffett demonstrates a washing machine. The store was located on Wilson Boulevard in Clarendon. (AHS.)

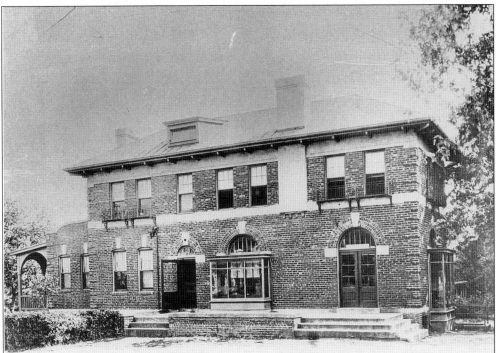

The C & P Telephone office in Clarendon, shown in 1920, replaced the Rosslyn switchboard, which had been established by the Falls Church Telephone Co. in 1900. The old facility had 50 lines, one of which ran to a single phone on a party line serving the courthouse. When the new Clarendon office was built in 1920, Arlington had 750 phones. (AHS.)

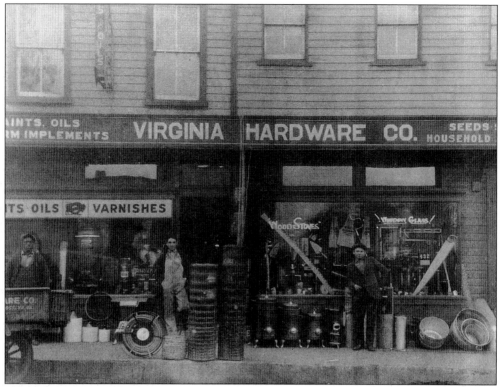

Virginia Hardware at 2016 N. Moore Street in Rosslyn was operated by Harry Goldman, with his brother and Henry Anderson, an African American who died three years after the store opened in 1924 and was greatly mourned by the Goldmans and customers. In 1963-1964 the store moved to 2915 Wilson Boulevard in Clarendon, where it still operates. (ACPL.)

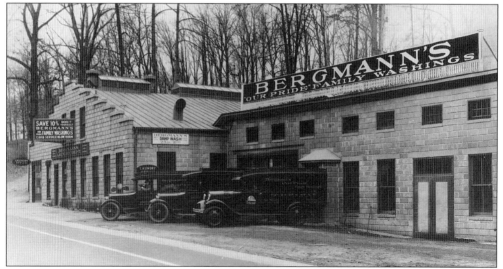

Bergmann's Laundry and Dry Cleaning started out in Washington in 1917 as a family-run business. Soon a plant was added in Arlington on Lee Highway, not far from Rosslyn and across from the Colony House store. This photo depicts the plant in 1920. The current location is the main headquarters for the firm. (AHS.)

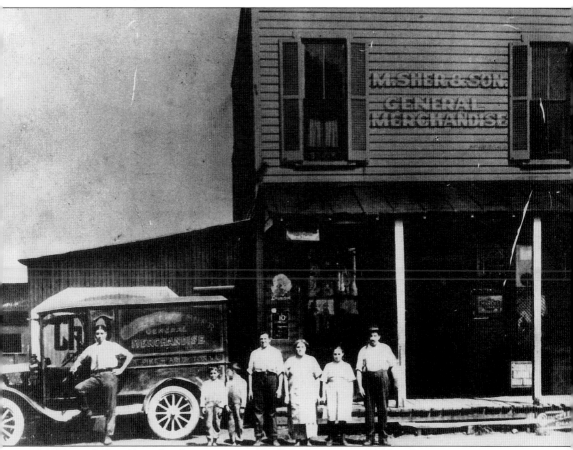

Members of the Sher family are pictured after they acquired the former C.F. Burner's Emporium. They are, from left to right, Charlie (at truck), twins Hyme and Joe, Abie, Esther, Ida, and Menashe. The earlier store was established in 1904 on Columbia Pike and the Nauck-Rosslyn line trolley tracks, which became Walter Reed Drive. The building was demolished between 1937 and 1939 by the building's owner, Dr. Charles Munson, to build the Arlington Theater (now Arlington Cinema 'N' Drafthouse). The Shers' business relocated across Columbia Pike. (ACPL.)

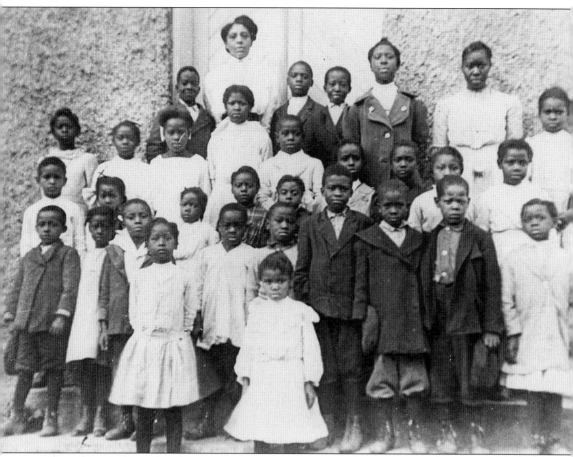

St. John's Baptist Church, on Columbia Pike at S. Scott Street, was established in 1903 and built in 1908. At that time, children living on the north side of the Pike had to cross it to attend a school on the other side. Their concerned parents petitioned the school board, which agreed to subsidize a school if a building could be found. The board rented the Sunday school room at the church and provided teachers, and the school, called St. John's Public School, operated c. 1910-1913. The first class at St. John's, shown here, included teachers Marie Wilson Syphax and Emma Holmes Clifford. Some of the students in the class (but not identified in the photo) were Thelma Cox Boswell, Audrey Cox Brown, Eula Cox Glass, Katherine Moseley Ross, Virgie Ward, and Eunice Madison Lee. When St. John's closed, the children attended Jefferson School. (AHS.)

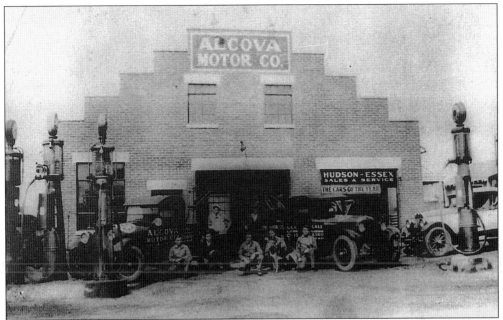

Alcova Motor Co., shown here in 1927-1928, was located at 3601 Columbia Pike, and the building lives on today as the Broiler (see Chapter Six). Post office directories of the 1950s and 1960s list this as a general auto repair shop, indicating the shop also did frame straightening and welding. (ACPL.)

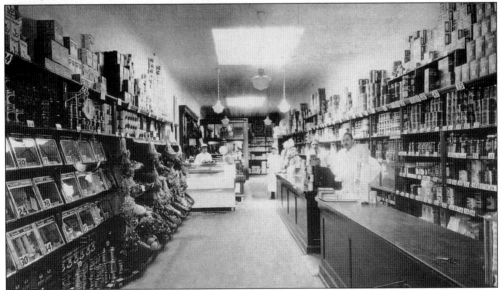

The Arlington Hardware, near the intersection of Columbia Pike and Walter Reed Drive, is a landmark business in South Arlington that was sorely missed when the store closed due to fire in 1996. It reopened in 1997, operated by Nora Gabaldon, daughter of the founder, and her husband David. The business was established in 1937 on Columbia Pike by David Eisen and moved to its current location in 1955 when he bought a grocery (shown here) and the adjoining drug store. His store carried appliances, toys, and records. Today, a third generation of the family is carrying on the store's reputation of kind and helpful service. (ACPL.)

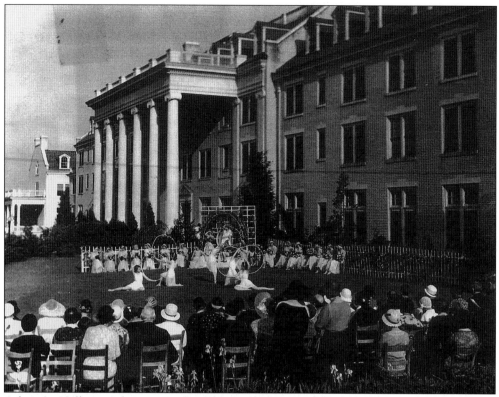

Arlington Hall, on Arlington Boulevard between George Mason Drive and Glebe Road, was chartered by Virginia as a junior college in 1927 and opened that fall with 35 students. It later was a high school and junior college that served local students and others from around the country. By 1941, there were 202 students. It was seized in 1942 during the National Emergency and became a secret cryptologic center (1945-1976) and a U.S. Army intelligence center (1977-1989). In 1985, legislation was enacted to transfer land to the State Department for a Foreign Service training school and to the National Guard. The main building shown here was preserved. (ACPL.)

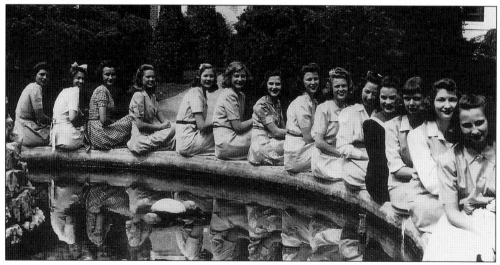

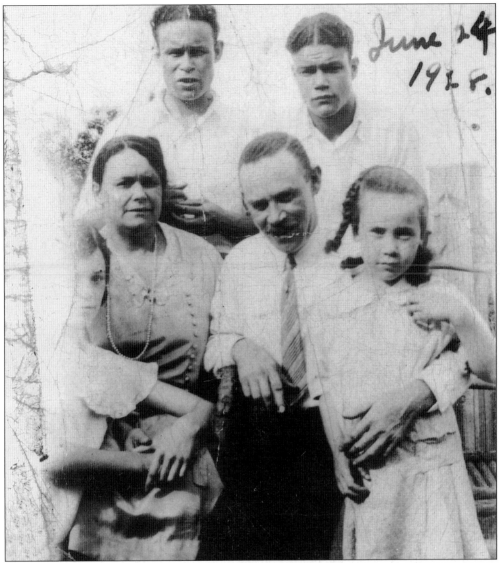

June 24 1928.

The Drew family was photographed in June 1925 in the yard of their home at 2505 First Street, S. The Drews moved from Washington in 1920. The Arlington home became the Drew homestead and has been lived in by four generations of the family. The house is listed in the National Register of Historic Places and the Virginia Landmarks Register and is a National Historic Landmark. Charles, who became a noted athlete, research scientist, and surgeon (see Chapter Four), is standing to the left in the photo, next to his brother Joseph. He attended Stevens Elementary School in Washington until 1918 and, like many other Arlingtonians in the 1920s, continued to go to D.C. for schooling, graduating from Dunbar High School in 1922. (Drew.)

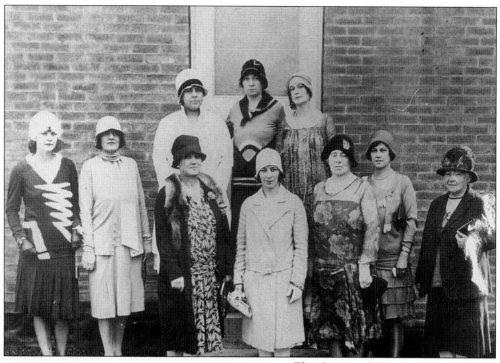

The Organized Women Voters of Arlington are shown in a 1928 photo. Founded in 1923 as the League of Women Voters, the organization was actively involved in improving the community through the promotion of better jail conditions, better health facilities, and more sanitary schools. The organization remained active into the late 20th century. (AHS.)

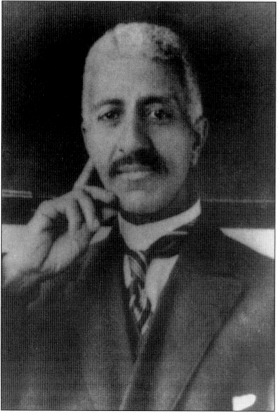

Edward C. Hoffman was a principal of four-room Jefferson Elementary School, located on S. Queen Street in the Arlington View neighborhood, formerly Johnson's Hill. The building was altered in 1930 to become a high school. The name was changed to Hoffman-Boston, after Mr. Hoffman and Miss Ella M. Boston, former principal of Kemper School, established in 1881 in the Nauck community. The Hoffman-Boston building is now the Hoffman-Boston Elementary School. (ACPL.)

The Little Tea House, located on Arlington Ridge Road and depicted here in 1927 postcards, was for more than four decades a world-famous gathering place of notables. One might have seen diplomats or Amelia Earhart, who would come up from nearby Hoover Airport. It has been said that more important world decisions probably were consummated there than in Washington. It was built in 1920 and closed in 1963 to make way for an apartment building (see Chapter Five). (Saulmon.)

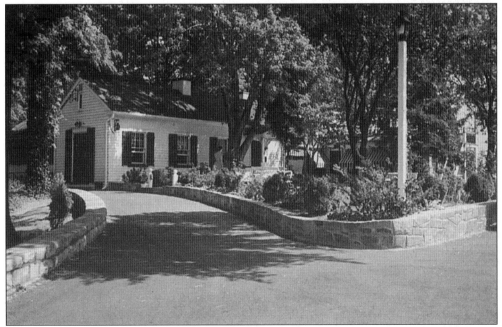

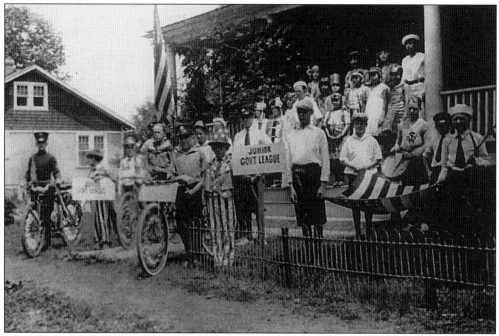

The Thrifton Village Junior Government League is shown here *c.* 1925 on the occasion of the July 4th parade in Thrifton. Thrifton included Maywood and part of Woodmont. This photo was taken in the 3200 block of N. Twenty-second Street in Maywood. James A. Shaw, who later became a Washington Senators baseball pitcher, is on the left. The league was heralded by local newspapers as a successful youth experiment through participation in self-government and discipline. (ACPL.)

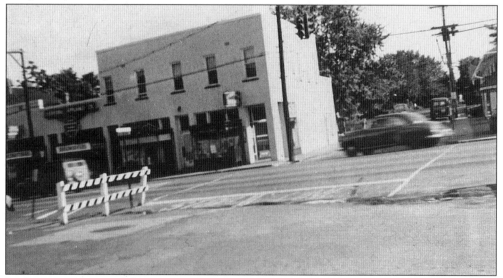

In this *c.* 1930 view of the N. Quincy Street and Lee Highway intersection looking south on Quincy, the corner building housed the Cherrydale Pharmacy that opened in 1920. The other shops included a variety store and a gift shop. The barricade is on land once used as a right-of-way by the Washington and Old Dominion Electric Railway Co. that came through Cherrydale and went on to Great Falls via Old Dominion Drive. (AHS.)

"Grandmother" Dudley stands beside the well house at her Cherrydale home in 1925. Most houses in Arlington had to rely on wells or springs for water until a county water supply was turned on in 1927. The house was heated by wood stoves and lighted by kerosene lamps until 1926, when electricity was put in. (AHS.)

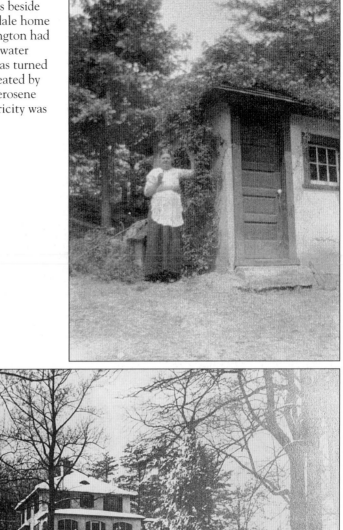

This 1928 photograph shows the home of John G. Dudley, a lawyer, and his wife, Mary. Located on Military Road, the house was on the site of the present Cherrydale Library, which was built in 1961. Mr. Dudley was chief of steamboat inspection service for the U.S. government and a special assistant to President Herbert Hoover. He also was a founding member of the Cherrydale Masonic Lodge. (AHS.)

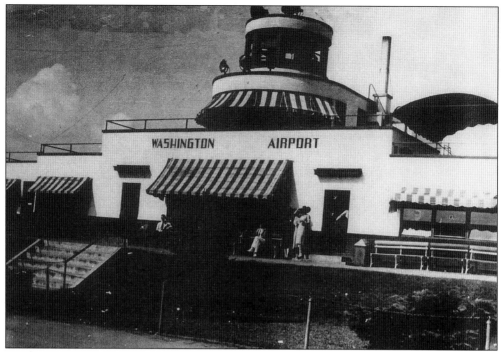

Washington Airport opened in 1927 on land at the south end of the Highway Bridge (later known as the Fourteenth Street Bridge) adjacent to Hoover Airport, which had begun operations a year earlier. The owners of Washington Airport, developers R.E. Funkhauser and Herbert Fahy, also founded Seaboard Airlines, which operated a small fleet of eight-passenger aircraft. Daily round-trip service to New York was offered beginning in 1928. In 1930, the owners of both airfields sold out to the National Aviation Corporation of New York, which combined the two and named the enlarged facility Washington-Hoover Airport. (ACPL.)

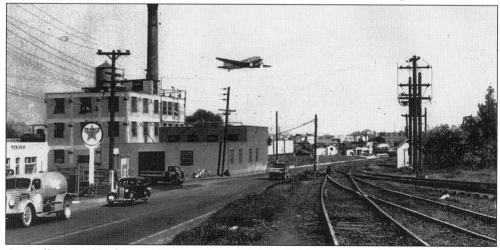

Air traffic using Washington-Hoover Airport in the 1930s encountered a number of hazards, some of which are seen in this photo. In 1934, a pilot was killed when his aircraft hit the power lines next to Route 1 not far from this spot. An even more serious obstacle, however, was S. Washington Boulevard, which crossed the sod runway. In 1941, Washington-Hoover Airport was replaced by Washington National (now Reagan National) Airport. (ACPL.)

Four

HOUSING, GOVERNMENT, AND THE WAR YEARS: 1933–1945

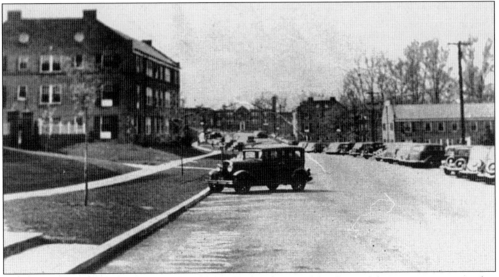

Colonial Village, constructed between 1934 and 1940, was the first garden apartment complex constructed in Arlington County and one of the first such complexes in the United States. It also was the first large-scale rental project to be approved by the Federal Housing Administration for mortgage insurance and became a model for similar developments throughout the nation. (AHS.)

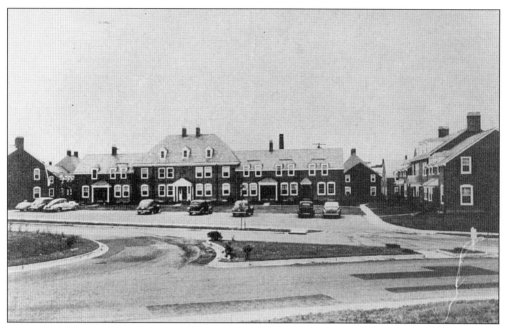

Fairlington, a garden apartment complex constructed between 1942 and 1944 in Arlington and Alexandria, is a nationally significant example of large-scale, publicly financed housing built for defense workers and their families during World War II. It was the largest apartment complex in the nation at that time. (AHS.)

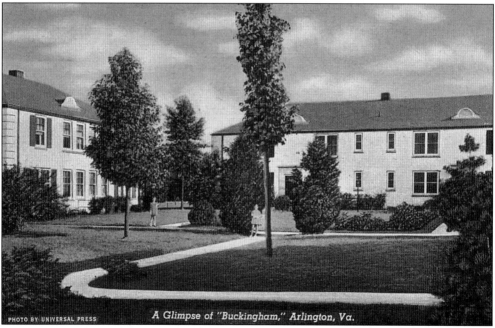

PHOTO BY UNIVERSAL PRESS   *A Glimpse of "Buckingham," Arlington, Va.*

Buckingham, a garden apartment complex constructed primarily between 1937 and 1941, is a nationally significant example of the application of the pioneering principles of garden city planning to a large, residential community. (Baker.)

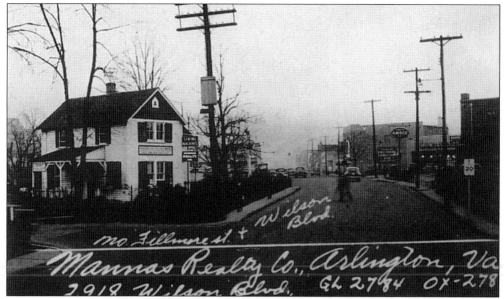

This post-World War II view of Clarendon looking west along Wilson Boulevard from Fillmore Street shows Mannas Realty Co. Wilson Boulevard has been an important transportation artery since the 18th century when it was called Awbrey's Road. Construction of the electric railway, around 1900, led to commercial development around Clarendon Circle and construction of homes for workers commuting to Washington. (Daniel.)

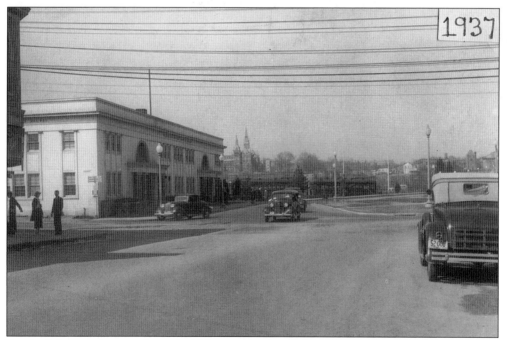

Rosslyn's history dates to the early 18th century when John Awbrey's ferry operated across the river from this location. This 1937 photo was taken at the Virginia end of the Francis Scott Key Bridge, which replaced the old Aqueduct Bridge. A trolley is shown at its terminal, and across the river are the spires of Georgetown University. (AHS.)

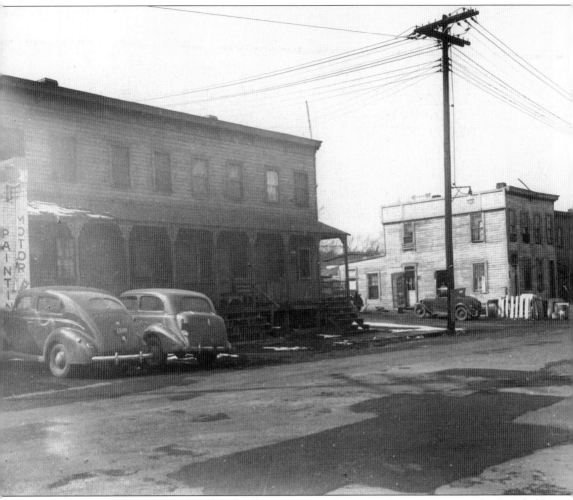

When this photograph of Rosslyn's "Pork Chop Row" on Fort Myer Drive was taken, probably in 1940, small businesses dominated the area. The notorious saloons of an earlier period had been eliminated through the efforts of Commonwealth's Attorney Crandel Mackey and newspaperman Frank Lyon. (AHS.)

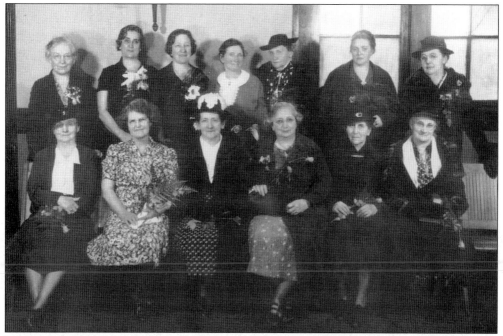

Virginia Compton's Grandmother Club was formed in 1934 when Mrs. Compton's first grandchild was born. She is second from the left in the front row. Others in the picture are a Mrs. Tabor, Emily Snarr, a Mrs. George, and a Mrs. Sigmundson, whose son was an Arlington County policeman. (ACPL.)

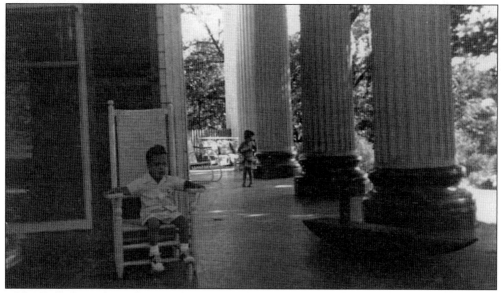

Altha Hall, formerly Ruthcomb Hall, was a splendid Greek Revival house, completed in 1889 on the site of Fort Strong, near Lee Highway and N. Adams Street. The original owner was Andrew Adgate Lipscomb, an assistant district attorney for the District of Columbia during the Cleveland administration. From the 1930s until sold to developers, the house served as a nursery school and kindergarten operated by Miss Anna Payne. It was demolished in 1959. (ACPL.)

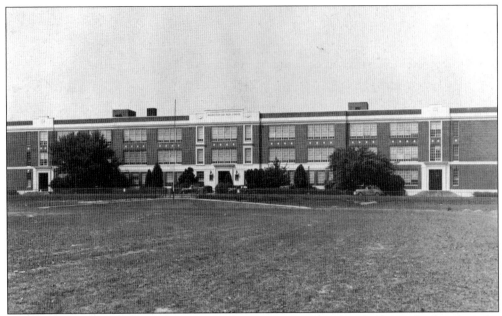

Washington-Lee High School was opened in 1925 to serve the children who lived in the northern part of the county, many of whom had previously attended high school in the District of Columbia. Other high schools, Mount Vernon and George Mason, were in an area annexed by Alexandria in 1929. Wakefield High School opened in 1953 and Yorktown High School in 1960. (AHS.)

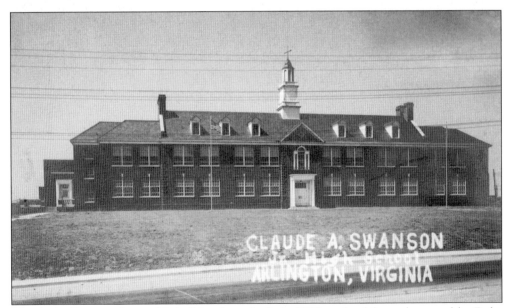

Claude A. Swanson Junior High School was built in 1939 on land formerly owned by Duke Torreyson adjacent to Westover, then known as Fostoria. Later a middle school, the building was named for a man who was successively a congressman, a governor, a senator, and Secretary of the Navy. (Baker.)

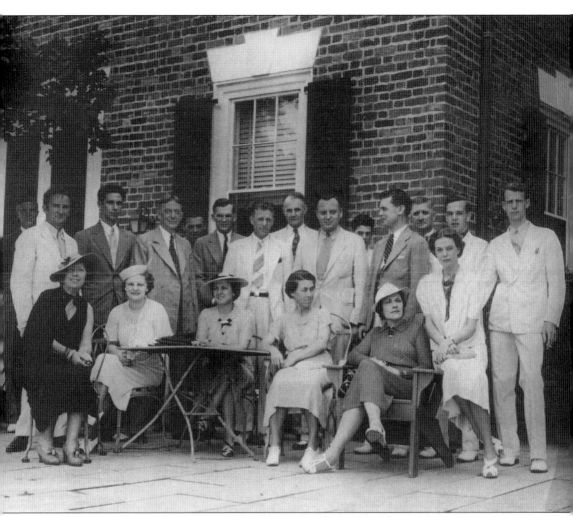

Pictured at a hotel in Culpeper, VA, in 1937 are members of a delegation to a meeting of Republicans. Among those standing, beginning fifth from left, are Grayson Ahalt, John Locke Green, Clarence Ahalt, and Bryan Gordon. Bryan Gordon Jr. is at the far right. Fourth from left is Henry Styles Bridges, a newly elected senator from New Hampshire. Among those seated is Tillie (Mrs. Clarence) Ahalt, fourth from left. Frank G. Campbell is standing third from right, his wife, Mary, seated third from left. Mr. Campbell was a founding member of the Washington law firm of Shepherd and Campbell, a founder and director of Metropolitan Savings and Loan Association in Arlington, and a president of the Civic Federation of Arlington. Mr. Green, a lawyer, served as Arlington County treasurer from 1940 until 1951. (ACPL.)

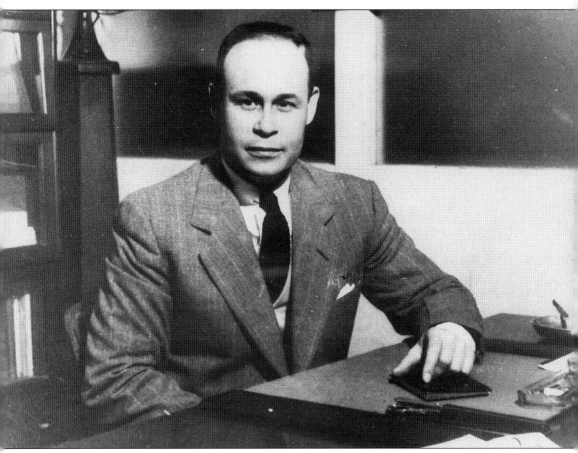

Charles Drew (1904–1950) was a physician whose laboratory discoveries resulted in the development of techniques for preserving blood plasma. He taught at Howard University Medical School and was the founder of the American Red Cross blood bank. His home in Arlington has been listed in the Virginia Landmarks Register and the National Register of Historic Places. It also is designated a National Historic Landmark. (AHS.)

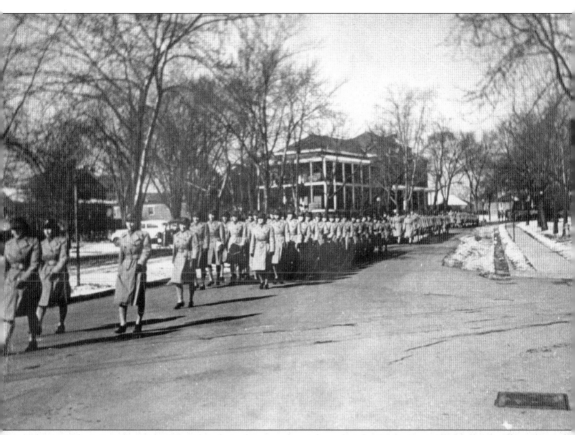

The parade ground at Fort Myer has long been a showplace for the U.S. Army's Third Cavalry and the colorful Old Guard (Third Infantry). Shown here is a less traditional parade—the Women's Army Corps parading during World War II. These women freed men for combat tasks. They also were believed to save the Army money. It was estimated that, because women ate less than men, the Army could save $2.7 million a year! (AHS.)

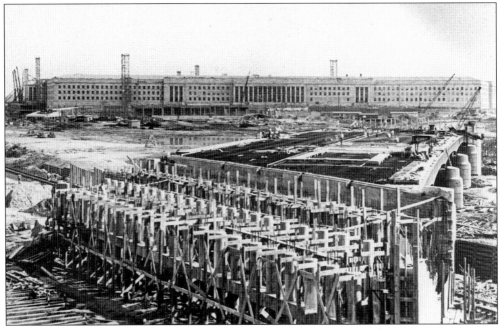

Construction of the Pentagon began in October 1941 to consolidate War Department employees scattered throughout Washington. Work proceeded rapidly and was completed in January 1943. It was the largest building in the world, accommodating more than 30,000 military and civilian personnel, who were part of the influx of workers to Arlington during World War II, doubling the county's population in three years. (AHS.)

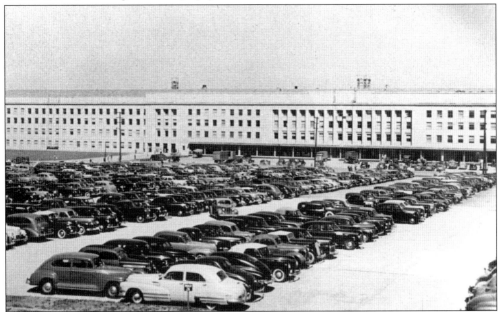

The completed Pentagon, shown in this c. 1944 photo, occupied a 320-acre site and included parking for 7,000 cars as well as 30 miles of approach roads, cloverleafs, and overpasses. Construction of the complex destroyed several Arlington neighborhoods—Queen City, East Arlington, and South Arlington. (AHS.)

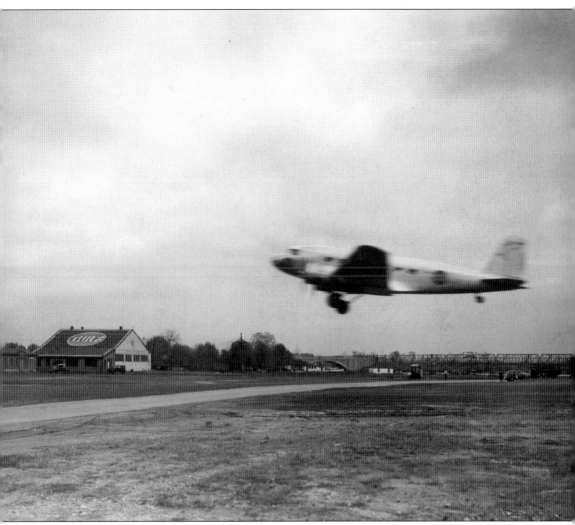

An Army Signal Corps photo shows a plane taking off at Hoover Airport in 1935. S. Washington Boulevard, running across the airfield, had to be closed off with chains during takeoff and landing, because sirens proved ineffectual with drivers using the road. Another hazard for flyers was a burning dump nearby that sometimes filled the air with dense smoke. (AHS.)

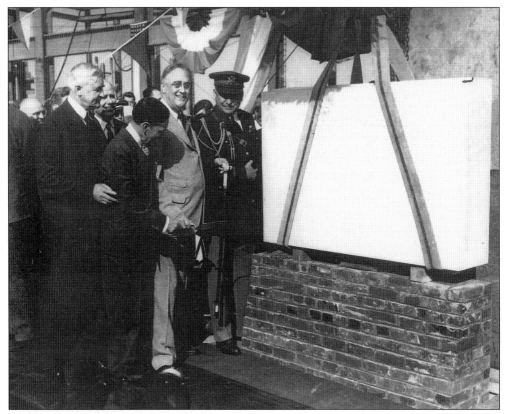

Smiling broadly, President Franklin Roosevelt stood erect, trowel in hand, as he laid the cornerstone for Washington National Airport in September 1940. Legislation for replacing the inadequate Hoover Airport, which opened in 1926, had been introduced in Congress in 1927, but disagreement over the location resulted in a stalemate until 1938, when Roosevelt intervened and selected an area by the Potomac River near Gravelly Point, the southern end of Alexander's Island. A lot of dredging and excavating was necessary to make the site level and solid. (ACPL.)

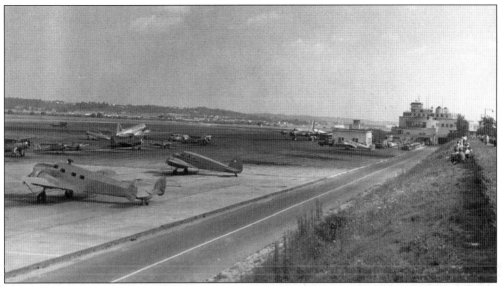

National Airport, which opened about five months before the bombing of Pearl Harbor, was already too small for the traffic it handled when this photograph was taken in 1946. Greatly expanding over the years, the airport authority created a furor among local historians in the 1990s when it proposed removing the ruins of Abingdon, which are on the airport grounds (see Chapter one). The ruins were saved, and the enlarged airport was renamed in honor of former President Ronald Reagan, who left office in 1989. (AHS.)

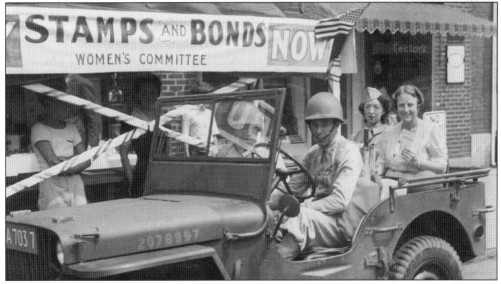

World War II and the growth of the military establishment had a tremendous effect on Arlington and its residents. From 1941 to 1944, the population grew from 57,000 to 120,000, placing increased demands on housing, child care, recreational activities, and public facilities. Residents recycled aluminum, participated in regional commissions for defense and protection, conducted air raid drills, volunteered for aircraft spotting, experienced rationing and shortages, opened their homes to boarders, and, as shown in this photograph, supported War Bond drives. Visible in the background is Rector's Flower Store, located at 3171 Wilson Boulevard in 1946, opposite the Ashton Theater. (AHS.)

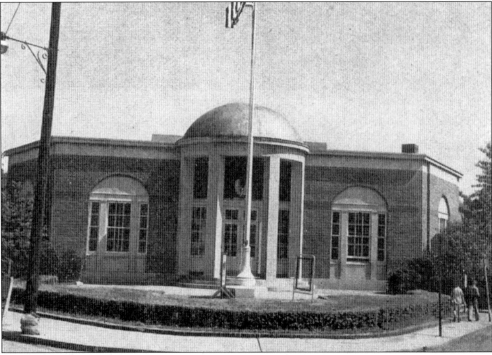

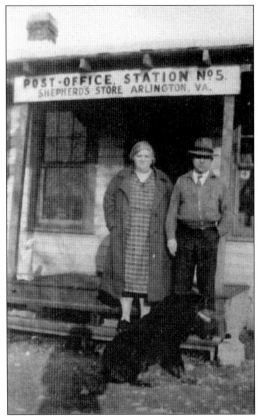

The Arlington, VA Post Office was established July 1, 1936. It consolidated and centralized mail delivery to the entire county, which had previously been accomplished by a number of smaller second- and third-class post offices serving local neighborhoods. The renaming of Arlington's streets about the same time, eliminating duplicate street names, also facilitated this effort. The cornerstone for this building was laid on May 5, 1937, using the same trowel used by George Washington to lay the cornerstone of the U.S. Capitol. (ACPL.)

Mr. and Mrs. Clyde Shepherd, shown here c. 1940, operated a store and post office in Glencarlyn. Located on S. Carlin Springs Road, the store and nearby house were sold in 1962. A convenience store and dry-cleaning establishment were constructed on the site. (ACPL.)

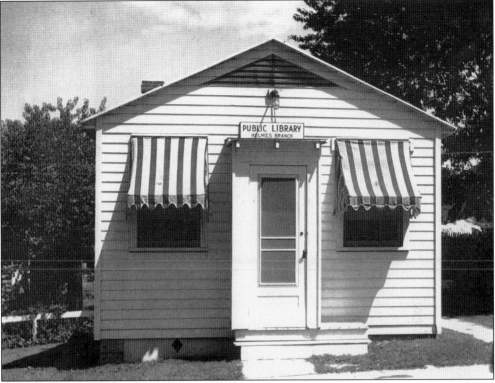

Organized in 1940, the Henry Lewis Holmes Library Association established a public library in the Sunday school room of Mt. Olive Baptist Church. Serving the African American members of the community in which it was located, the Holmes Library was named for a former resident who had been active in promoting civil rights. (ACPL.)

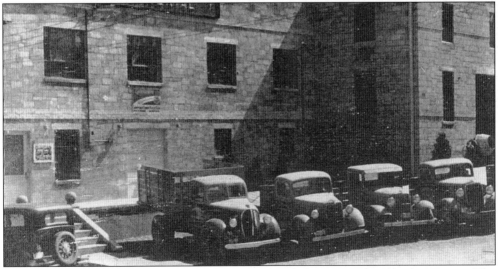

The Cherrydale Cement Block Company was founded in 1922 by Charles Toone. The company supplied blocks for water and sewer lines. Blocks from the company also were used to construct a number of houses in Maywood, Cherrydale, and other Arlington neighborhoods, as well as Washington-Lee High School. (ACPL.)

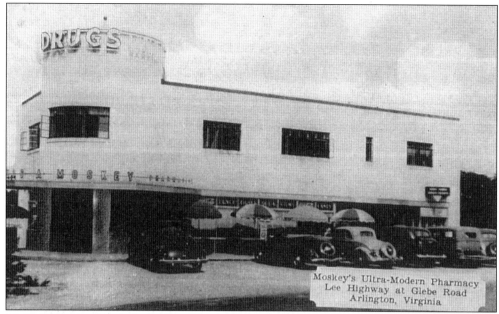

Moskey's Pharmacy was located at the intersection of N. Glebe Road and Lee Highway in the 1930s. In more recent times, the building has housed a number of banks. (Chaves.)

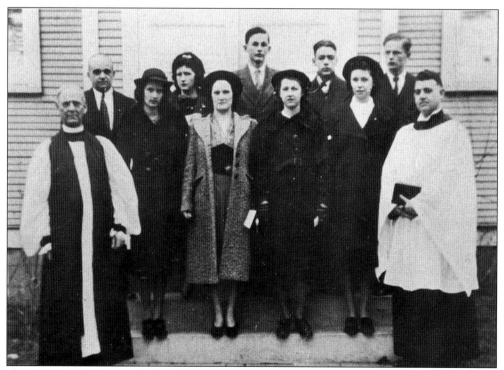

This is a confirmation class at Epiphany Episcopal Church in the 1930s. The church on Ballston Avenue (later N. Stuart Street) in Cherrydale is believed to have been built in 1914-1915. The congregation later moved to St. Andrew's Church on Military Road. Rev. Sparks was rector at both Epiphany and Trinity Episcopal churches in the 1920s. (ACPL.)

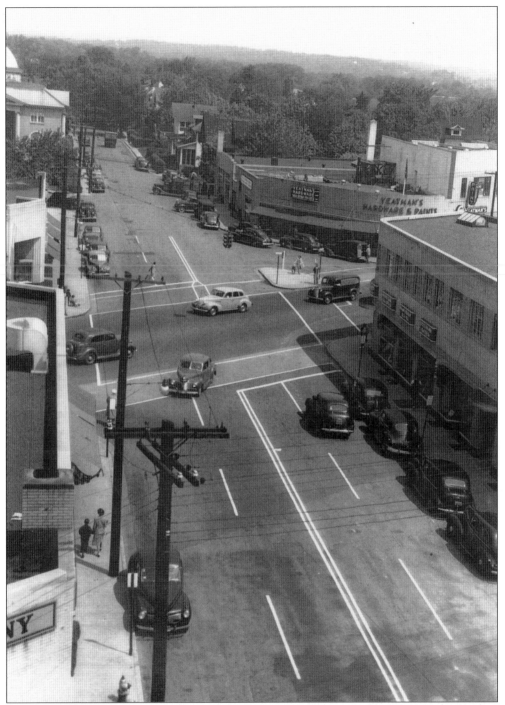

The intersection of Wilson Boulevard and N. Highland Street in Clarendon became a major center of commercial activities in the 1930s and '40s. The prominent businesses shown (now demolished) are Hahn's Shoes (white building on the left across intersection) and Yeatman's Hardware (opposite Hahn's). The First Baptist Church of Clarendon is in the upper left. The entrance to the Clarendon Metro Station now stands on the left side of the photo. (ACPL.)

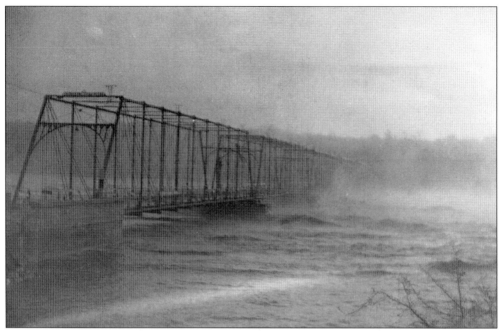

The pictured Chain Bridge (c. 1936–37) was the seventh of eight at this location. It was built in 1874 by the Army Corps of Engineers. It was flood-damaged and closed in 1927 until repairs were made in 1928. Flooding again damaged the bridge in 1936, and in 1937 a flood permanently closed it, resulting in construction of the present-day bridge, which opened in 1938. (ACPL.)

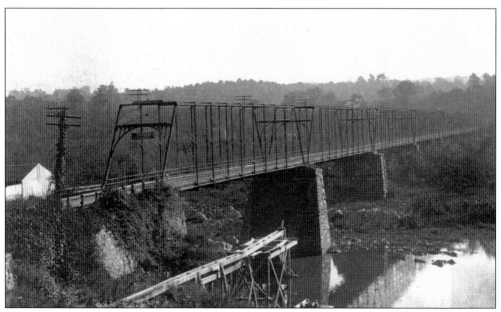

This picture of Chain Bridge from the Arlington side was taken between 1890, when electricity was first used at the bridge, and 1928, when the bridge abutment was reinforced with cement. A barge can be seen anchored in the river. There were a quarry and a stone-crushing mill at the bridge during this period. (ACPL.)

Five

FROM SUBURBAN TO URBAN: 1945–1970

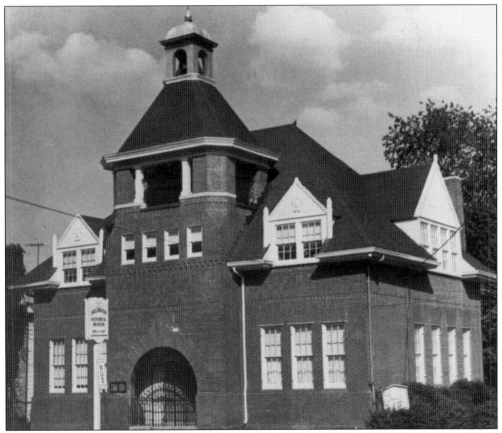

This is the former Hume School after it became the Arlington Historical Museum, owned and operated by the Arlington Historical Society. The museum, which opened in 1963, is self-supporting. It is open three days a week, staffed by volunteers, and houses a collection of many hundreds of artifacts related to Arlington County history. (AHS.)

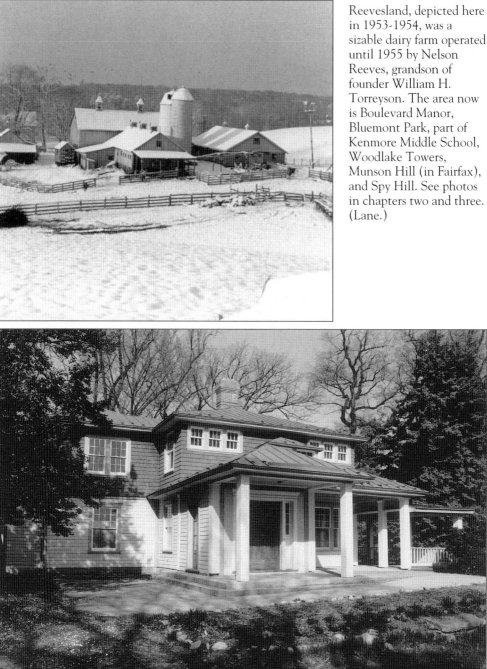

Reevesland, depicted here in 1953-1954, was a sizable dairy farm operated until 1955 by Nelson Reeves, grandson of founder William H. Torreyson. The area now is Boulevard Manor, Bluemont Park, part of Kenmore Middle School, Woodlake Towers, Munson Hill (in Fairfax), and Spy Hill. See photos in chapters two and three. (Lane.)

The Hendry house is located on the grounds of Fort C.F. Smith. The fort was erected during the Civil War to protect the approaches to the Aqueduct Bridge and the nation's capital. The house, built c. 1890, and the grounds were purchased in 1927 by Dr. Ernest S. Hendry, a horticulturist who planted numerous rare trees on the place. Today, the property is an Arlington County park. (ACPR/WO.)

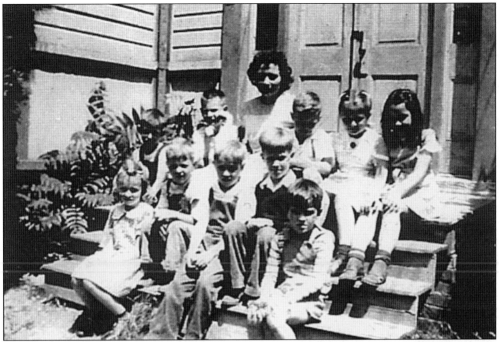

Teacher and pupils at Glencarlyn School gathered for a photo on the last day of school in the spring of 1948. The school met in Carlin Hall, shown in this photo. The Carlin Hall Association donated the use of its building to the school board in 1920, after the old school burned, and Carlin Hall housed Glencarlyn School for 30 years. (ACPL.)

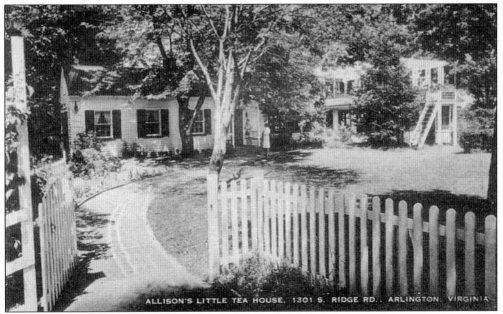

The Little Tea House, on Arlington Ridge Road, is described in chapter three. It was a Virginia and Washington institution for four decades until destroyed in 1963 to make way for an apartment building. Its stone well house east of the Arlington Historical Museum can still be seen. (Daniel.)

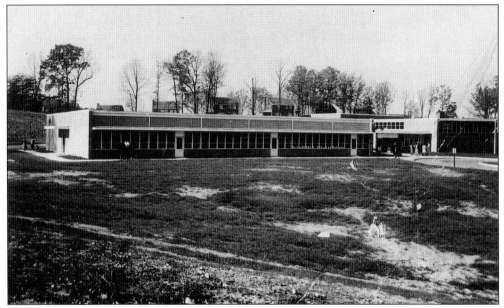

McKinley Elementary School, on McKinley Road near Wilson Boulevard, shown in this c. 1951 photo, was one of the first modern schools in Arlington built to meet the needs of the post-World War II baby boom. (McKinley.)

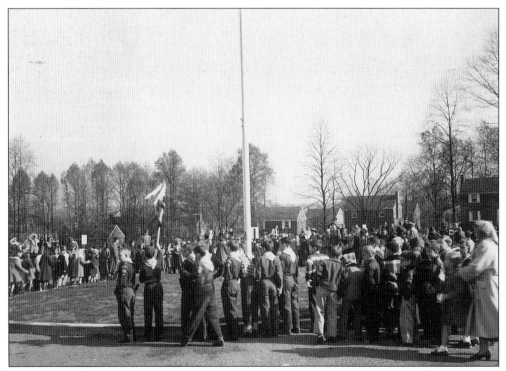

Students and parents at McKinley Elementary School observe Armistice Day, November 11, 1951. Armistice Day is now celebrated as Veterans Day. (McKinley.)

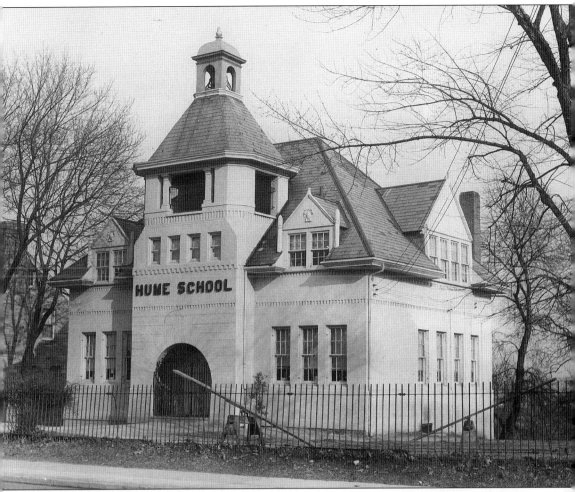

The Hume School, constructed in 1895, is the oldest standing school building in the county. It was named for Frank Hume, on whose land the school was built. Frank Hume was a distinguished business and political leader and Civil War veteran. The school was closed in 1956, and the building was donated to the Arlington Historical Society in 1960 for use as a museum. (AHS.)

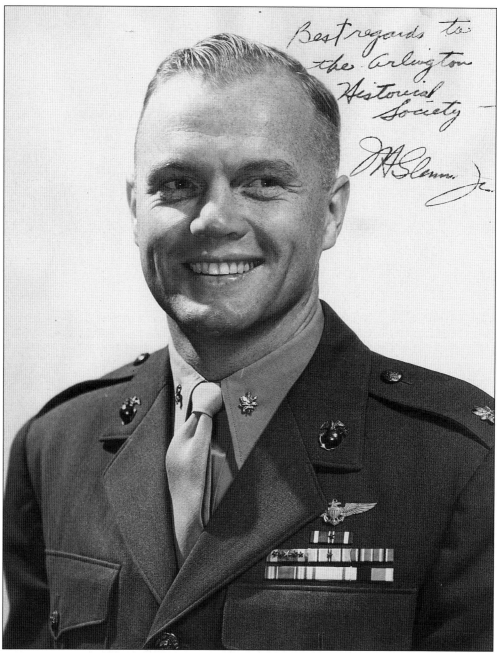

Best regards to the Arlington Historical Society —

J.H. Glenn, Jr.

Senator John Glenn, Jr., who in 1962 became the first American to be put into orbital space flight, was a resident of North Arlington. He was elected to the U.S. Senate from Ohio in 1974. (AHS.)

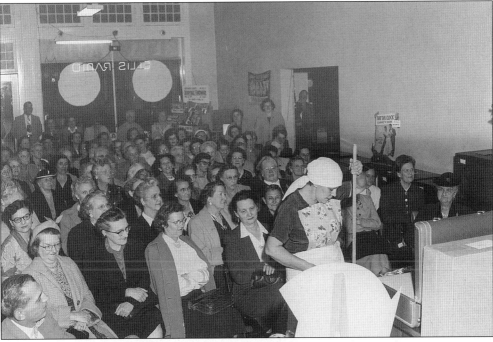

A representative of General Electric Company demonstrates modern washing equipment to Arlington homemakers in 1952 at the Ellis Radio shop on Lee Highway in Cherrydale. (AHS.)

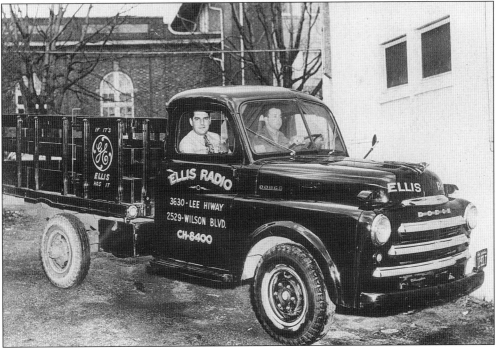

Joe and Cliff Ellis are sitting behind their store, Ellis Radio, on Lee Highway in Cherrydale in 1948. The building in the background is the old Cherrydale School. The Ellis family owned a second store on Wilson Boulevard in Clarendon. (AHS.)

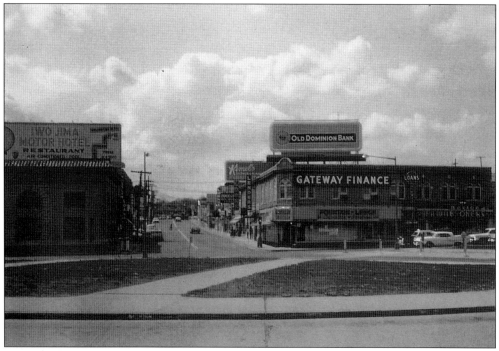

This view of Rosslyn in the late 1950s or early 1960s shows the area near Rosslyn Circle (foreground) before redevelopment began. (ACPL.)

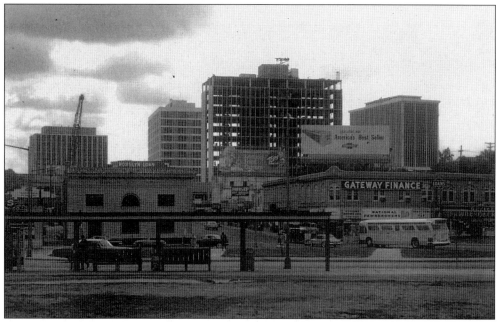

In the 1960s, when this photo was taken, the character of Rosslyn was changing. Once primarily a one-story business district of pawnshops and loan companies, several of which are visible, it was becoming a neighborhood of high-rise apartment and office buildings and hotels. In the foreground is the passenger waiting area at what was originally the Rosslyn Circle transfer point between the Washington trolley system and the suburban bus lines. (ACPL.)

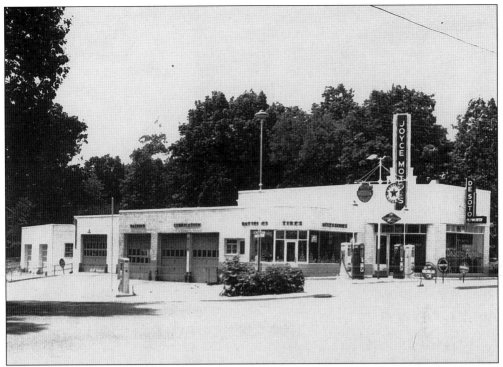

Joyce Motors, shown here in 1948, still occupies the same location on Tenth Street in Clarendon. (ACPL.)

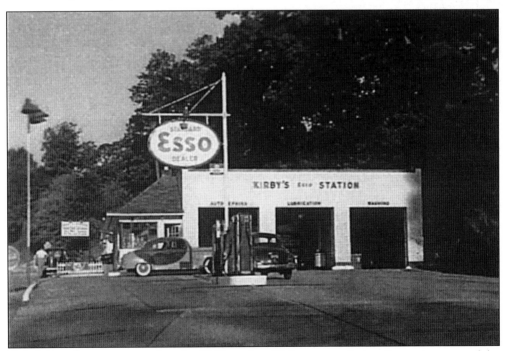

Kirby's Esso Station operated in the 1940s on Lee Highway near Irving Street, just west of the Lyon Village Shopping Center. (ACPL.)

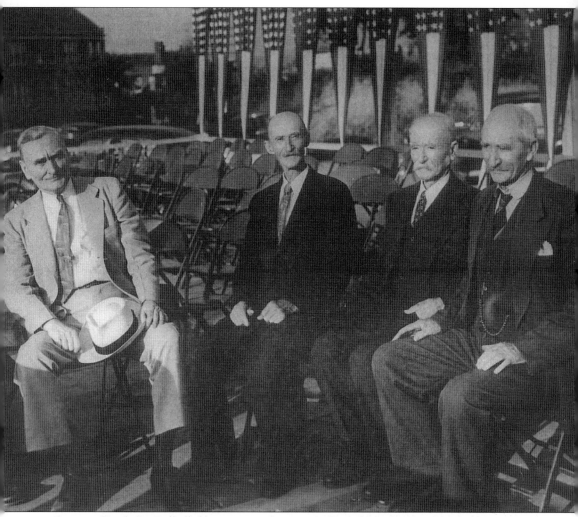

Senator Frank L. Ball (left) meets with some other old-timers at the 50th anniversary celebration in 1948 of the old county courthouse. Sitting with Mr. Ball are Philip Marcey (102 years old), John Marcey (100), and George Marcey (98). (ACPL.)

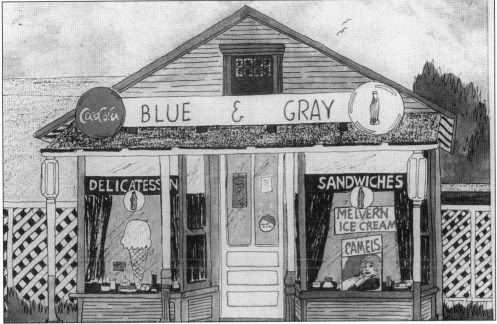

The Blue & Gray was a popular hangout and snack shop for Washington-Lee High School students. As the sign in the window shows, cigarettes as well as food could be purchased there, which concerned some of the parents. The shop earned a place in the Washington-Lee yearbook of 1946. (ACPL.)

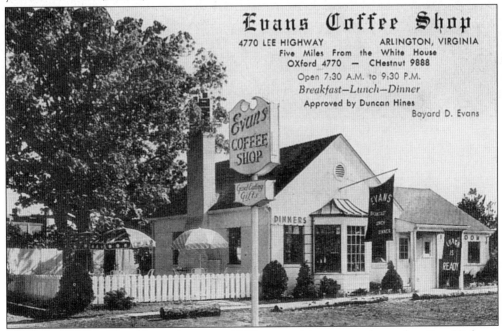

The Evans Coffee Shop, shown here in a 1957 postcard image, was located on Lee Highway near Glebe Road. Bayard and Ruth Evans of Evans Farm Inn fame operated this popular dining spot from at least the 1940s until 1961. It was succeeded by several eateries before becoming the Alpine Restaurant in 1966. (Baker.)

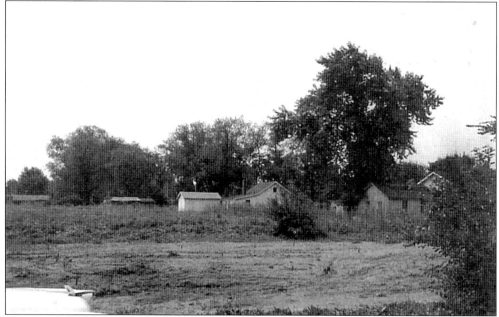

In 1958, Arlington County purchased this farm, located in the 1000 block of N. Quincy Street between Washington Boulevard and Fairfax Drive, as the site for the proposed central library. The county paid $62,500 for 2.41 acres to owners Libbie Burrows and Sarah E. Brown. (ACPL.)

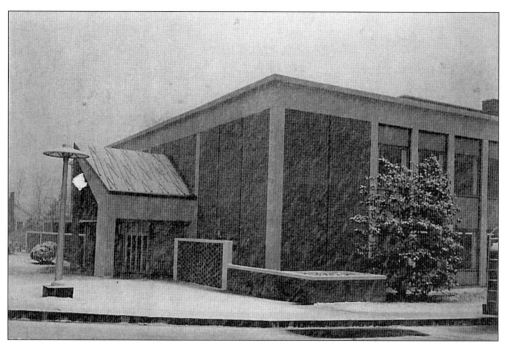

The Arlington Central Library, designed by J. Russell Bailey, was inaugurated May 14, 1961. It cost $520,560 to build. Mildred Blattner, library director from 1941 to 1957, and David Krupsaw, county board chairman, made major contributions to the construction of this milestone in Arlington's history. The building was renovated in 1992. (ACPL.)

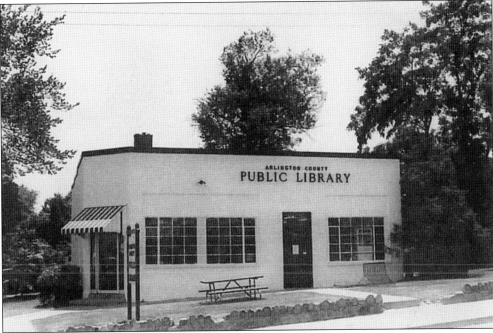

The Aurora Hills Branch Library, shown in 1969, was replaced by a new building that combines the library, a fire station, and a visitors' center. (ACPL.)

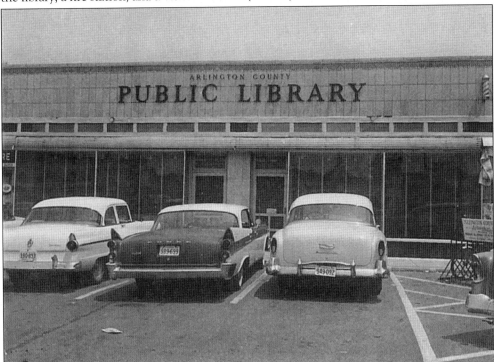

This branch of the Arlington County Library system, shown in 1959, was located on Columbia Pike. The new branch for this area is part of a building complex that includes other educational facilities. (ACPL.)

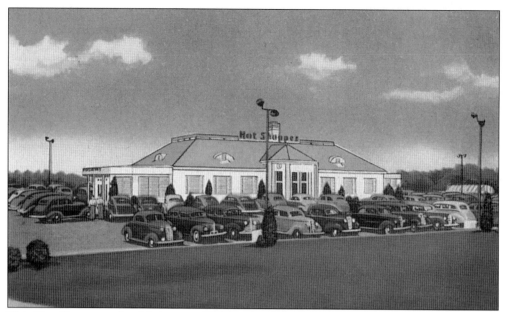

This Hot Shoppe on Lee Highway at Kirkwood Road near Lyon Village was one of a chain of these popular restaurants in the Washington area. In 1927, J.W. Marriott left his native Utah to come to Washington. Starting with a root beer stand, his business prospered, and by the 1940s and '50s he had several Hot Shoppe restaurants and cafeterias. (Baker.)

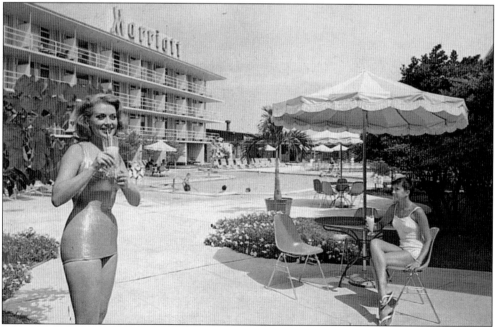

The Key Bridge Marriott, built in 1959, was one of the earliest modern hotels built in the redeveloped Rosslyn. Ideally located, it has been enlarged by several stories since this photo was taken. (Baker.)

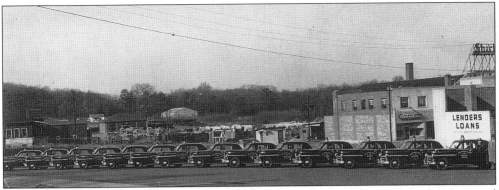

The Arlington Police Department was relatively new when this picture of the property yard near Shirlington was taken, probably in the late 1940s. Police functions were the responsibility of the sheriff until a police department, under the county manager, was created in the late 1940s. Harry Woodyard was appointed as the first police chief. (ACPL.)

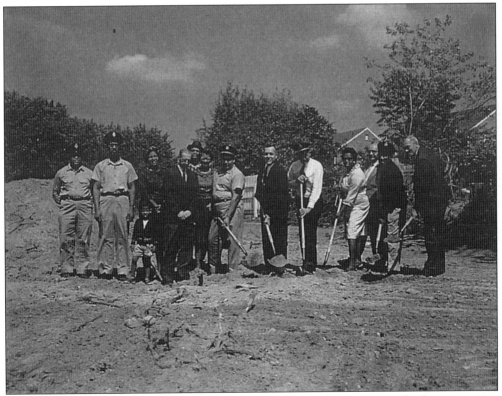

Before the 1930s, Arlington depended entirely on volunteer fire companies for fire protection. The Hall's Hill company, formed in 1918, was composed entirely of African Americans before integration became the law. This 1959 photo shows the groundbreaking ceremony for the new Hall's Hill station on Lee Highway. (ACPL.)

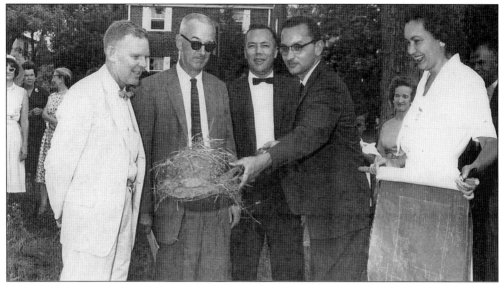

There were smiles all around at the July 1962 groundbreaking ceremony for the Westover Branch Library. Pictured are, from left to right, as follows: David Cine, chairman of the neighborhood civic association; Raymond Pelissier, president of the Friends of Arlington County Libraries; Leo Urbanske, Arlington County Board member; Thomas Richards, Arlington County Board vice-chairman; and Marcia Shufelt, Westover librarian. (ACPL.)

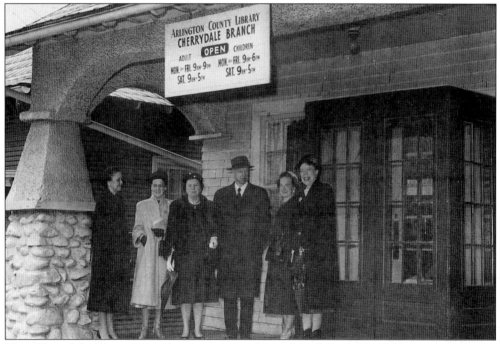

The Cherrydale Library's first home was the Cherrydale School. In 1938 it moved to the building shown here, formerly used as a clinic. That building was demolished in the 1950s to expand the intersection at Lee Highway and N. Quincy Street. The "new" Cherrydale Branch Library opened in August 1961. Jane Nida, longtime director of libraries, is second from right. (ACPL.)

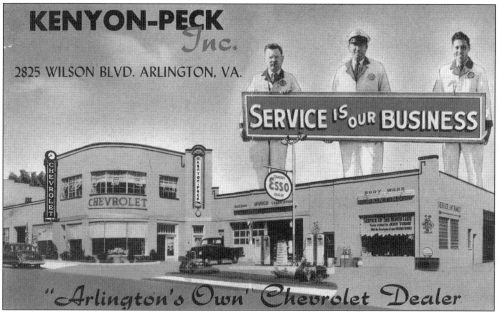

"Arlington's Own" Kenyon-Peck Chevrolet dealer was located in 1953 at 2825 Wilson Boulevard, two blocks from the heart of the Clarendon shopping district and directly across the street from the Sears, Roebuck and Company department store. The dealership boasted that their modern service department with factory-trained personnel was equipped to handle the automotive needs of all Arlingtonians. The dealership later relocated to the corner of Wilson Boulevard and Glebe Road. (Baker.)

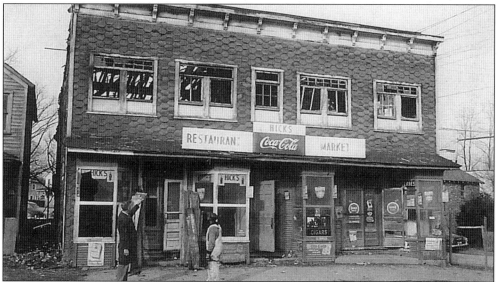

Hick's Store and Restaurant was located in Hall's Hill, named after a farm that belonged to Bazil Hall. The area became an African-American community after the Civil War. The family of merchant Theodore Hicks was buried in a graveyard that was condemned in 1959 for the widening of Lee Highway. Their remains were moved to a churchyard in Herndon. The family donated land for the nearby firehouse. The store continued in operation for many years and was replaced by a fried chicken restaurant. (ACPL.)

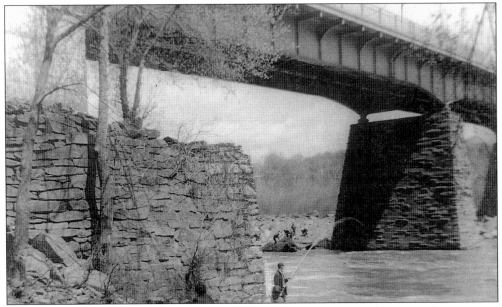

This spot at the first break in the Palisades below the Little Falls was an early river crossing. Two trails from the interior country met at this spot, and it is believed there was a Native American settlement and fishing ground here. Each spring, the herring and shad runs draw large crowds of fishermen to the area. (ACPL.)

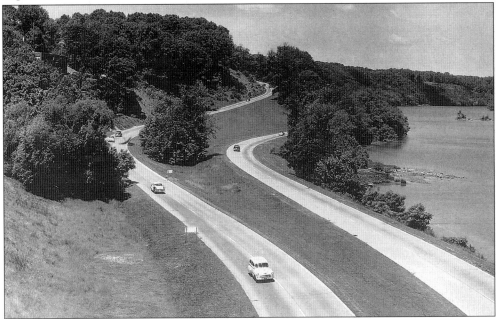

The George Washington Memorial Parkway's earliest section, from Memorial Bridge south to Mount Vernon, and then known as Mt. Vernon Memorial Boulevard, opened in 1932. It was extended north to Spout Run Parkway by 1950, and to the Central Intelligence Agency in Langley by 1960. In this view, looking northwest between Key Bridge and Spout Run, the Three Sisters Islands are on the right. They were the site of a controversial proposed bridge intended to carry I-66 across the Potomac. (ACPL.)

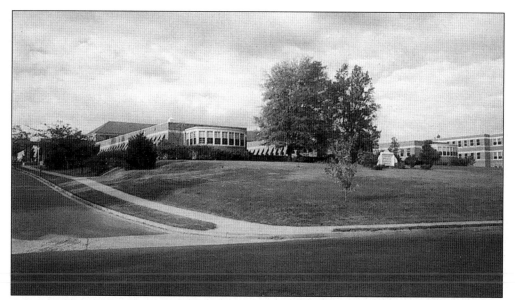

Arlington Hospital was built on the old Sealock farm, and its 15.5 acres were purchased in 1935 for $15,000. Ground was broken March 18, 1943, following approval by the Federal Works Agency, provided that no critical war materials (i.e., steel) were used in construction. The doors were opened to the first patients a year later. Although the federal government initially owned the hospital, the county purchased it after the war for $125,000. It has undergone many renovations and expansions since then. One postcard shows an architect's rendition of the proposed hospital, and the other shows the hospital soon after its construction. (McAtee.)

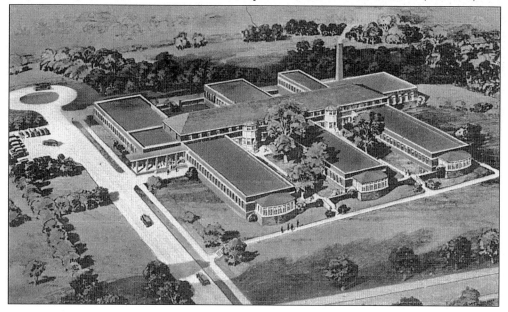

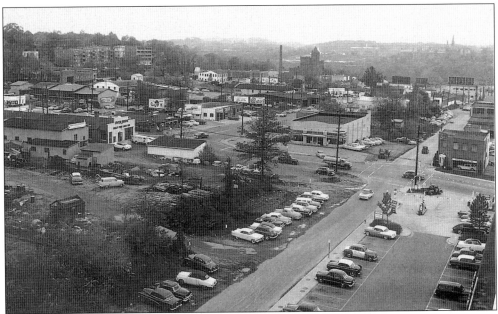

This late 1950s view of Rosslyn is looking toward the Potomac River and Georgetown. The large white building in the right center is the present-day Tom Sarris Orleans House restaurant, bounded by Lynn Street, Wilson Boulevard, and Moore Street. Dyer Brothers is the white square-front building in the center left. (ACPL.)

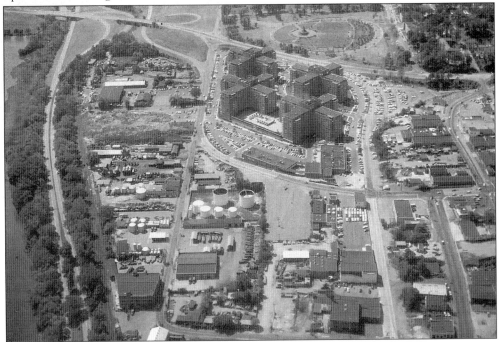

This view of Rosslyn in the late 1950s, looking south, shows the area before major redevelopment. The U.S. Marine Corps War Memorial (Iwo Jima) is in the circle at the top right. The four cross-shaped buildings were new apartments that were first called Arlington Towers (now River Place). (ACPL.)

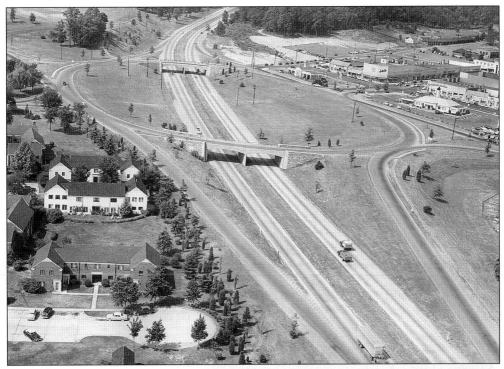

This 1959 aerial view of Shirley Highway shows Shirlington (upper right), Fairlington (upper left), and Park Fairfax (lower left). (AHS.)

The Henry G. Shirley Memorial Highway (I-395) was begun in the 1940s to relieve traffic congestion for Washington's wartime workers. This photo shows expansion of the highway near Glebe Road, 1950-1965. (ACPL.)

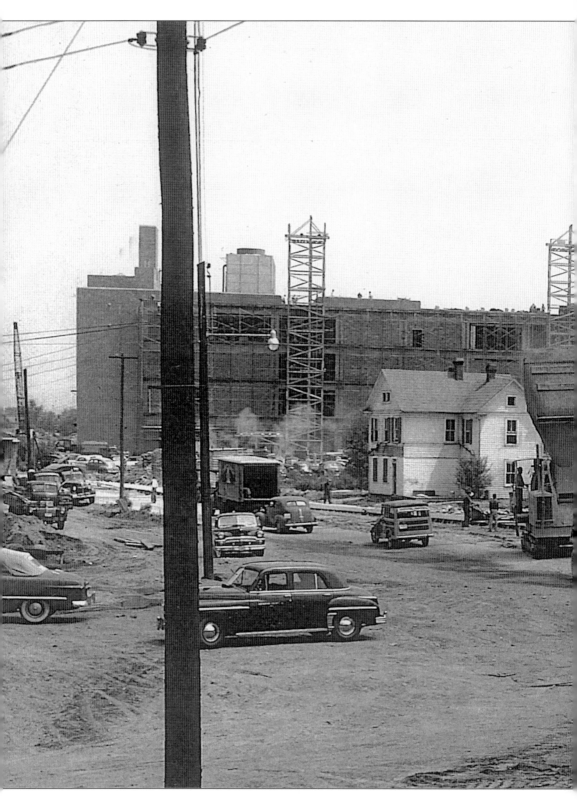

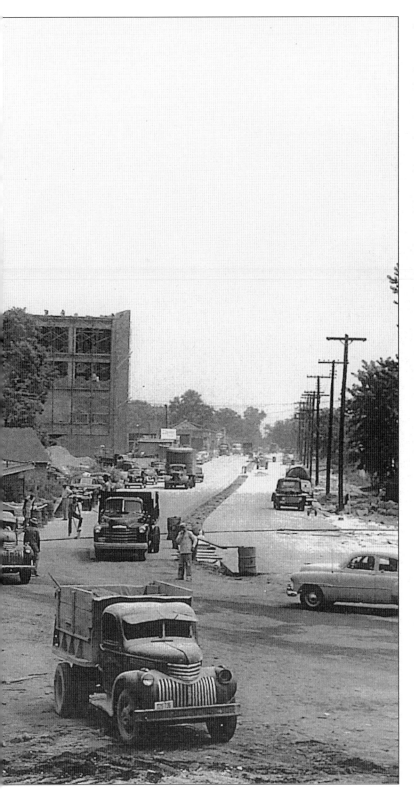

Once known as Birch's Crossroads, later Ball's Crossroads, and now known as Ballston, the area around the intersection of Wilson Boulevard and Glebe Road was called Parkington for a number of years beginning in the 1950s. This c. 1950 photo shows construction under way on the Hecht Company store, the major department store in the Parkington shopping center. (ACPL.)

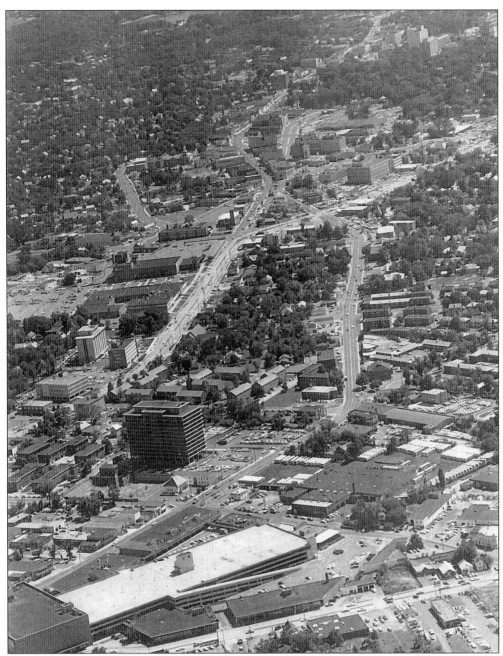

An aerial view shows Ballston, c. 1950, before major reconstruction in the late 1990s and early 2000s. Hecht's is at the bottom of the picture. Wilson Boulevard and Fairfax Drive lead to Clarendon Circle in the upper right. (ACPL.)

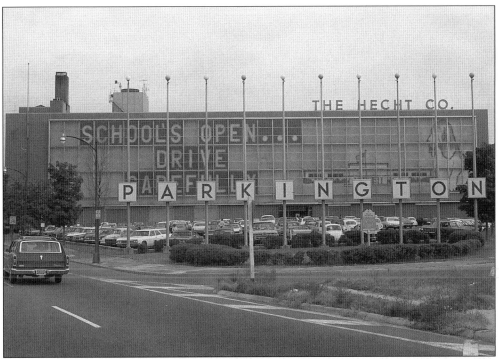

Perhaps the most famous feature of the Parkington Shopping Center, which opened on November 4, 1951, was the area's largest signboard. The solid glass facade of the Hecht's department store was 300 feet long by 50 feet high and was used to display holiday greetings and public service messages. (AHS.)

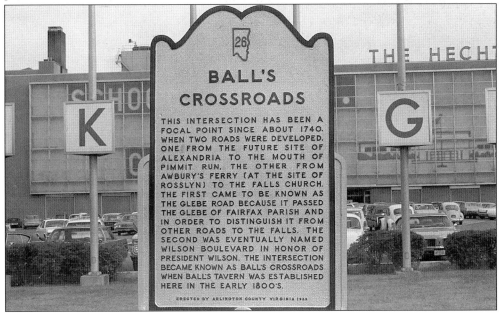

This historic marker, erected by the county at the intersection of Glebe Road and Wilson Boulevard, recounts the area's history. The Hecht Company's Parkington store is in the background. (AHS.)

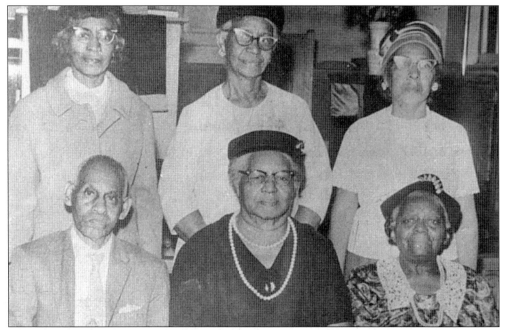

Members of the Calloway United Methodist Church Wesleyan Service Guild, pictured in 1966, were recognized for 50 years or more of service. Pictured, from left to right, are (front row) Claude Hyson, Ella Williams, and Josephine Brown; (back row) Viola Chase, Evelyn Wright, and Anita Showden. The church, located at 4800 Lee Highway, was founded in 1866 by residents of the Hall's Hill area. (AHS.)

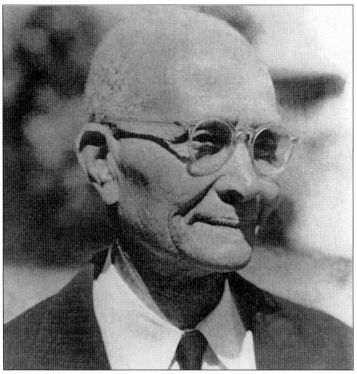

Park C. Syphax, a founding member of St. John's Baptist Church on Columbia Pike, was photographed in 1952 at the church's 50th anniversary celebration. He was the only surviving founder. (Syphax.)

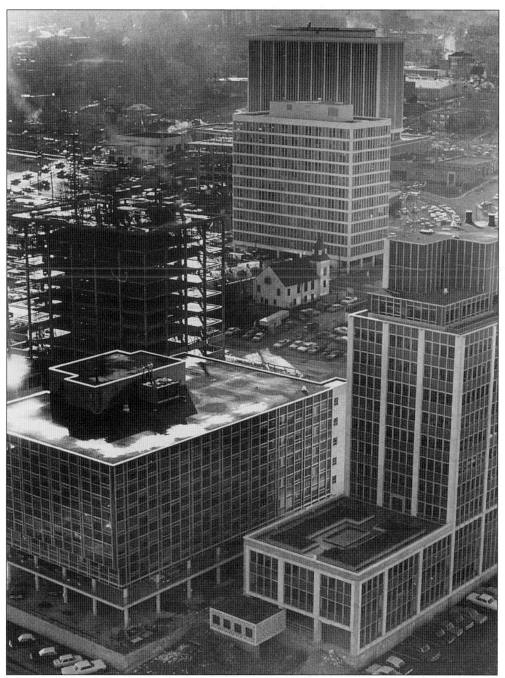

This c. 1964 view of Rosslyn, looking southwest, shows high-rise buildings replacing small business and residential areas. The small white building in the center was the First Baptist Church at 1827 N. Moore Street. The tall building at the top and center was the first high-rise constructed in Rosslyn. (AHS.)

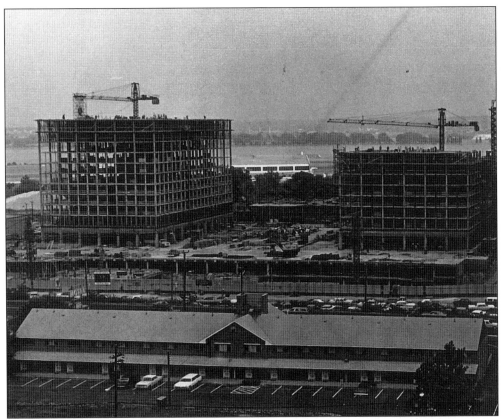

Construction of the Crystal Plaza high-rise on Jefferson Davis Highway (Route 1) was under way when this photo was taken in 1967-1968. The area now called Crystal City, near Reagan National Airport and north of the Potomac Yards, had been primarily industrial before it was developed by Charles E. Smith Realty Companies. (ACPL.)

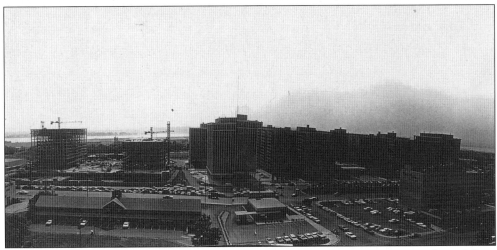

This panorama, probably taken in the early 1970s, shows ongoing construction in Crystal City. This area, once a series of brickyards, is now a mix of modern office and apartment buildings and home to a number of defense contractors, thanks to its proximity to the Pentagon. (ACPL.)

Six

REDEVELOPMENT AND DIVERSITY: 1970–2000

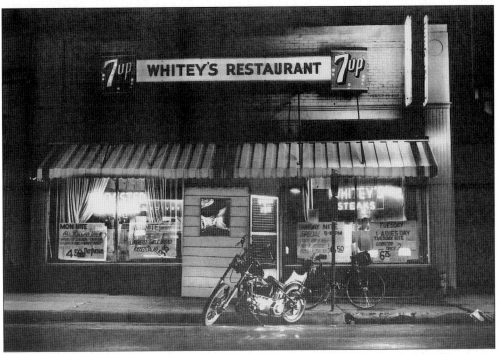

Whitey's Restaurant, shown c. 1980, has been a longtime Lyon Park landmark. The first owner, Alexander Joy, opened a bar and restaurant on N. Washington Boulevard near Pershing Drive. It became known as Whitey's because of Mr. Joy's white hair. The current owners bought the business in 1977 and doubled it in size. The outside of Whitey's hasn't changed. The neon "Eats" and "Broasted Chicken" signs remain on the front window. (ACPL/PD.)

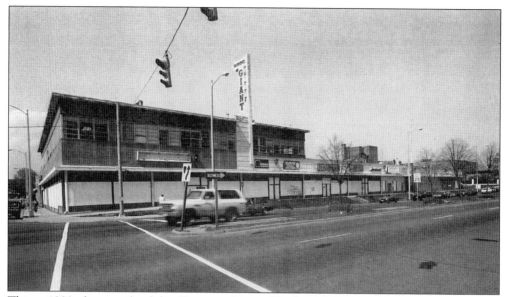

This c. 1980 photograph of the Giant market on Fairfax Drive was taken before the Federal Deposit Insurance Corporation complex was built. Adjoining Giant is a block of smaller businesses. In the background is S. Kann Sons department store, built shortly after World War II. In 1976, the Kann's building was leased to the International School of Law, which merged with George Mason University in 1979. The heritage of this shopping area gave Virginia Square Metro stop on the Orange Line its name. (ACPL.)

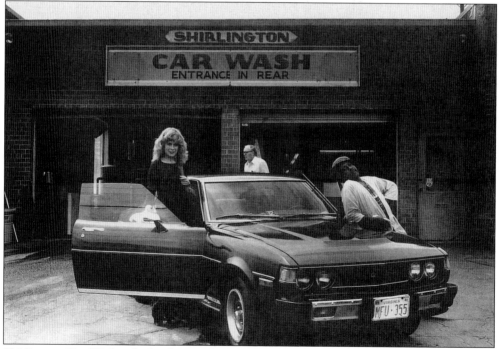

Shirlington Car Wash, which advertised as a "full service car wash with special equipment for van washing," was located at 2720 S. Arlington Mill Drive, in the Shirlington shopping center. These happy customers were photographed c. 1981. (ACPL/PD.)

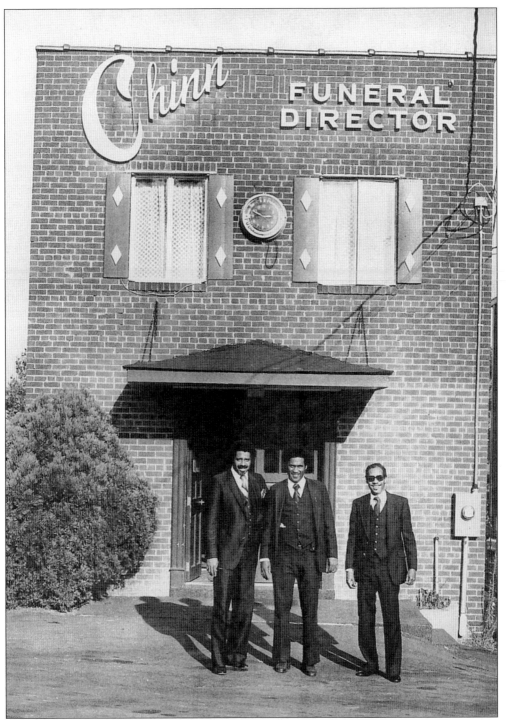

James E. Chinn, funeral director, opened his business in 1946 on S. Seminary Road, which was renamed Shirlington Road. In 1957, he moved to a new structure on the other side of the street. Robert Baker, who purchased the business in 1969, is the center figure in this 1970s photo. Franklin Brewer (now deceased) is on the left and Archie Pretty on the right. (ACPL/PD.)

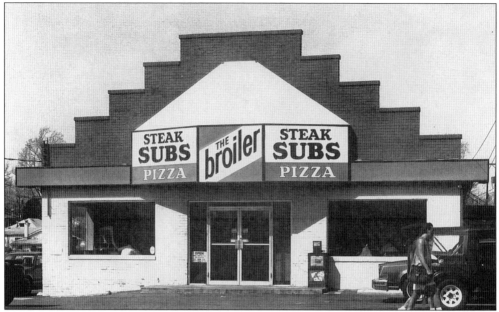

The Broiler at 3601 Columbia Pike has long been a popular eating and meeting place for local residents. Owner Irvin Zetlin first operated the restaurant at 3415 Columbia Pike from 1959 to 1972. In 1966, he bought the Alcova Motors property (see Chapter Three) and moved the Broiler there in 1972. Irv's father had owned a delicatessen and a grocery (Igloo) on the other side of Columbia Pike from 1946 to 1968. This area of the county along the Columbia Turnpike (or Pike) and its post office were called "Arlington" before the county adopted that name, and it has a long commercial history. (ACPL, with permission from Milton Schoch, photographer.)

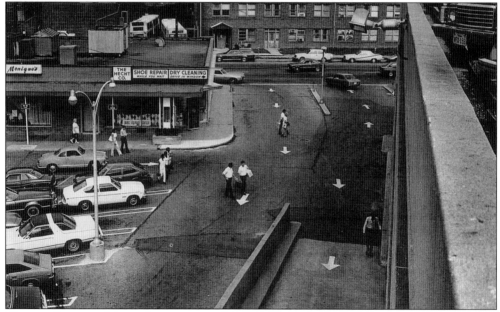

This small group of shops that was part of the Parkington shopping center was photographed between 1979 and 1981. The shops were demolished when the Ballston Common Mall was built at the Parkington site. (ACPL/PD.)

112

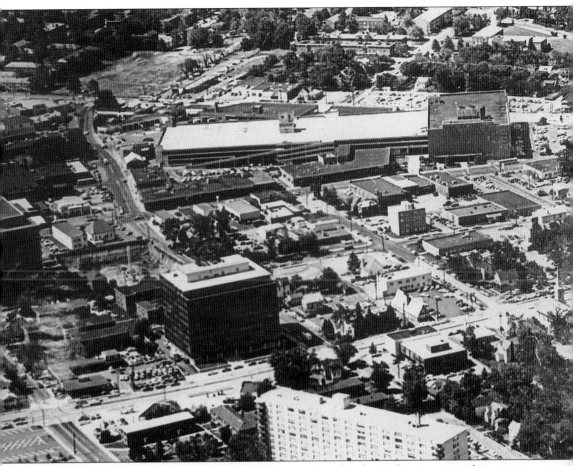

This 1970 aerial photo of Ballston (looking west and north) shows the area, once known as Ball's Crossroads, before the 1979 opening of the Metro station, which changed the community into one of towering buildings and busy streets. In the upper center is Parkington, a shopping center built in the early 1950s and later enlarged and renamed Ballston Common. The Metro station would be located near the center, on Fairfax Drive. (AHS.)

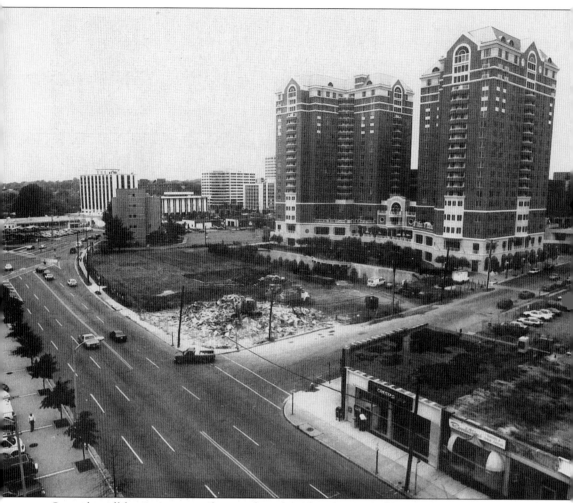

Several small businesses were destroyed to clear this site on Wilson Boulevard in Ballston for construction of a building to house the National Rural Electric Cooperative Association. Best known was the Putt-Putt Golf Course, a popular landmark for Arlington residents. The building in the background is a Marriott retirement home, the Jefferson. (ACPL.)

This 1987 photo is of the intersection of Quincy Street and Fairfax Drive, where a trolley stop named Utopia was once located. It was cleared for a proposed Metro stop; however, plans changed and the Metro station was never built. A large office building now stands at the location. Arlington Central Library is in the background. (ACPL.)

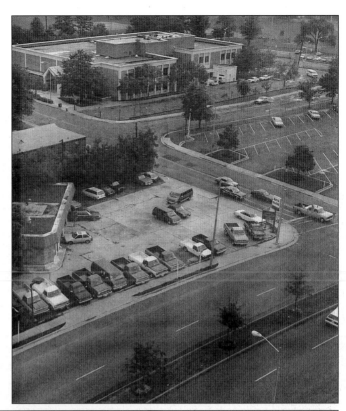

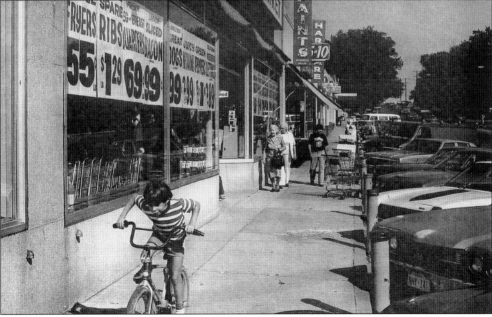

Westover shopping center, on N. Washington Boulevard and N. McKinley Road, has been a longtime Arlington neighborhood landmark. Arlington's last remaining five-and-dime store, Ayers, is in the center. John W. Ayers opened the store in 1948 and ran it for almost 30 years. The photo was taken between 1979 and 1981. (ACPL/PD.)

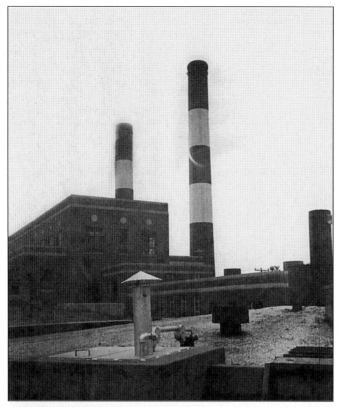

These smokestacks at the Arlington incinerator on S. Glebe Road were longtime Arlington landmarks. They were demolished in January 1985. (ACPL/DE.)

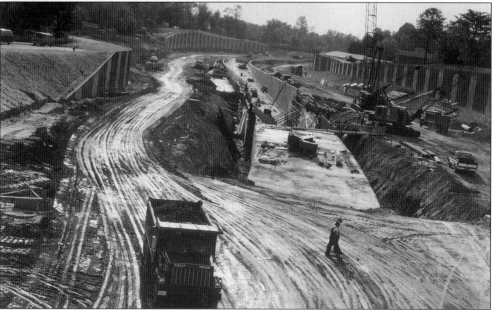

This photo shows construction of I-66 and Metro in 1980 at the point where the Metro surfaces between the Ballston and East Falls Church stations, near George Mason Drive. In July 1977, the first segment of Metro opened in Rosslyn, and Metro continued to East Falls Church in 1986. (ACPL/GS.)

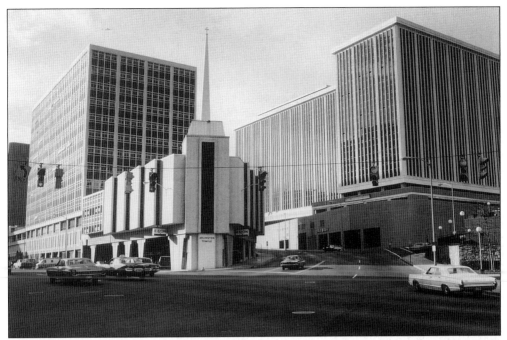

The Arlington Temple United Methodist Church and Community Center, built above a gas station at N. Nash Street and Fort Myer Drive in Rosslyn, was dedicated in November 1967. It fulfilled a dream of William P. Ames that part of the land from the Murphy and Ames lumberyard be set aside for worship, study, and social activities. (ACPL/GS.)

This construction sign is at the site of the Rosslyn Metro station, which opened in 1977. Bus service into many parts of Northern Virginia then terminated at the Rosslyn Metro station, which was on both the Orange and Blue lines, greatly increasing traffic and congestion in Rosslyn. Two years later, the Orange Line was extended to Ballston, which also became a bus terminal. (ACPL.)

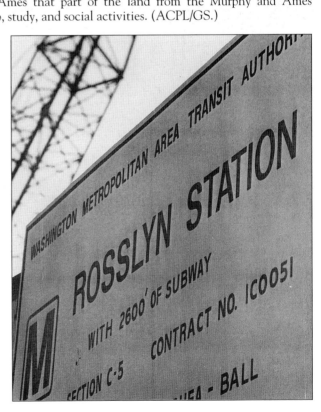

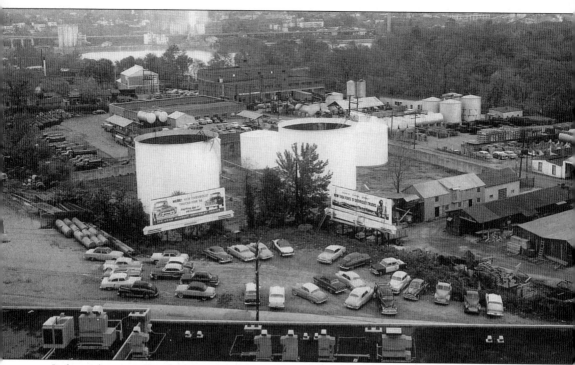

Industrial uses in Rosslyn continued into the 1980s, particularly in the eastern section above the George Washington Memorial Parkway. Note the tank farm. Today, all of that has been replaced, primarily by three high-rise office buildings in the vicinity of Wilson Boulevard and N. Lynn Street and by I-66. By the late 1980s, Rosslyn had become almost entirely an area of high-rise structures, and some older high-rises already were slated for redevelopment to greater densities and heights. (ACPL/PD.)

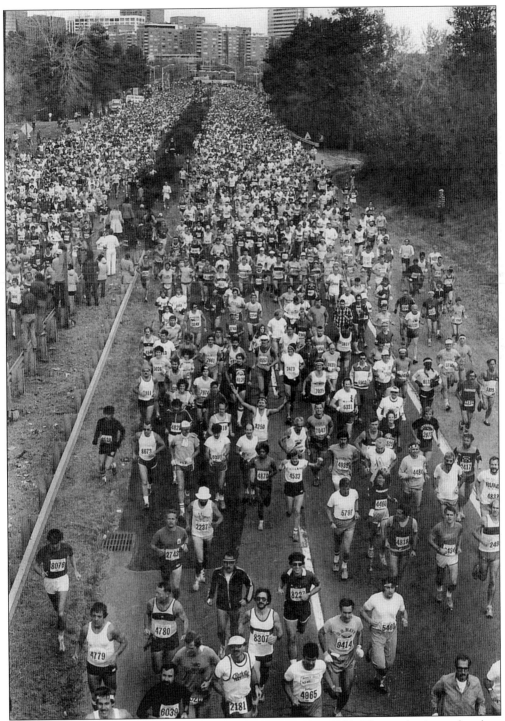

The first U.S. Marine Corps marathon was run in November 1981. The run begins and ends at the U.S. Marine Corps War Memorial (Iwo Jima) in Arlington, with a route through Washington. The largest number of participants has been 25,000 runners. Rosslyn is in the background. (ACPL/PD.)

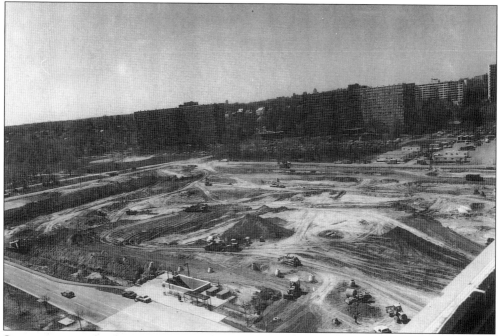

Site preparation for the construction of Fashion Center was under way when this photo was taken in April 1988. The area was once called Pentagon Valley. The Pentagon City Metro stop is in the foreground, and two River House apartment buildings are in the background. (ACPL.)

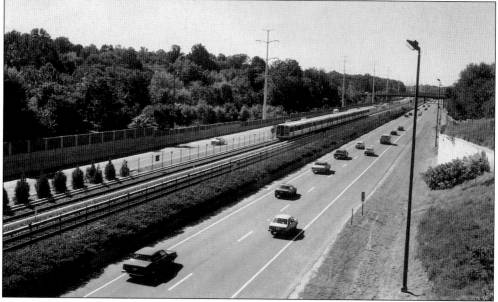

This 1986 photo shows the completed section of I-66 and Metro between Ballston and East Falls Church, looking west from Patrick Henry Drive. The Ohio Street bridge is in the distance. Interstate 66 connects with I-81 west of Washington near Front Royal, VA. Metro's Orange Line, seen here, runs to Vienna, in Fairfax County, VA. Metro's Blue Line runs from Washington through Arlington to Arlington Cemetery, the Pentagon, and Crystal City, and south to Springfield, VA, also in Fairfax County. (ACPL/GS.)

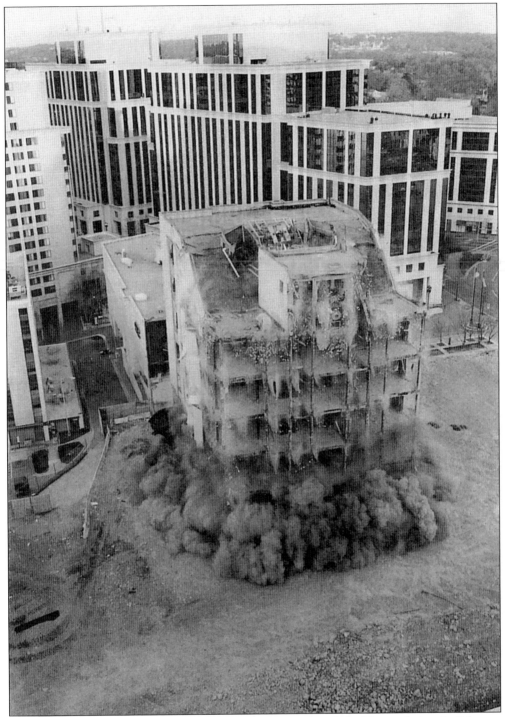

Arlington County's courthouse, dedicated in 1961, was demolished by implosion in February 1997. Controlled Demolition and Driggs Construction companies were employed for the task. An 1898 brick courthouse had been demolished and replaced by this building. The county's new administration building is behind and to the right. (ACPL/DE.)

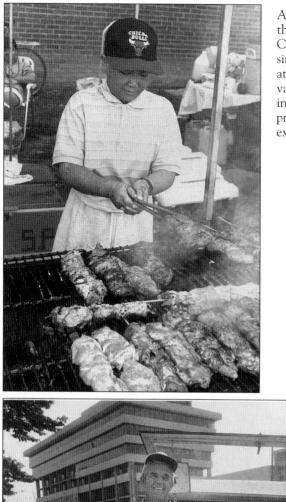

A very young vendor prepares food, in this undated photo, at an Arlington County Fair, an annual Arlington event since 1977. One of the fair's most popular attractions has been the ever-increasing variety of food to sample, especially international dishes, which often are prepared in a traditional manner by large, extended families. (ACPL/DE.)

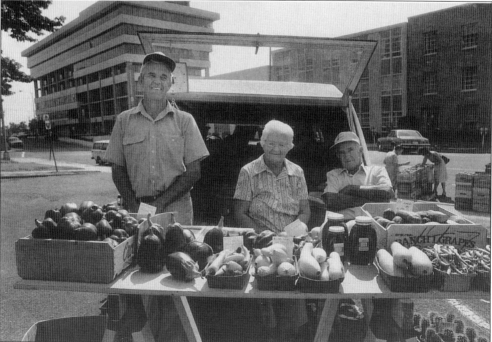

Three proud producers display their wares at the Arlington farmers market, c. 1980. (ACPL/PD.)

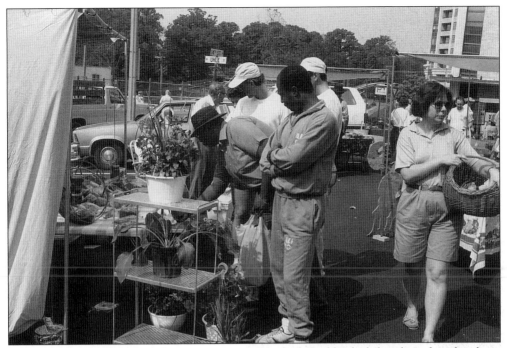

At the Arlington farmers market, a woman carries a basket of food while others shop for plants and flowers. (ACPL/DE.)

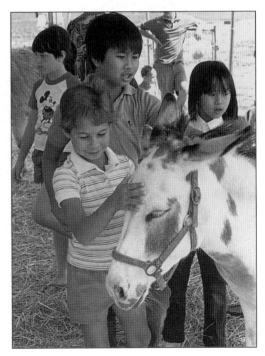

These children make friends with animals at the Arlington County Fair, held each year in August. (ACPL/DE.)

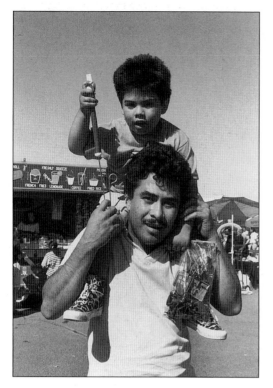

A father and his son are enjoying a day at the Arlington County Fair. (ACPL/DE.)

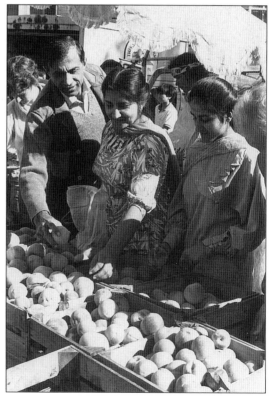

Reflecting the changing face of Arlington, three women select produce at the county's farmers market in the Arlington Courthouse parking lot. The photo was taken between 1979 and 1981. (ACPL/DE.)

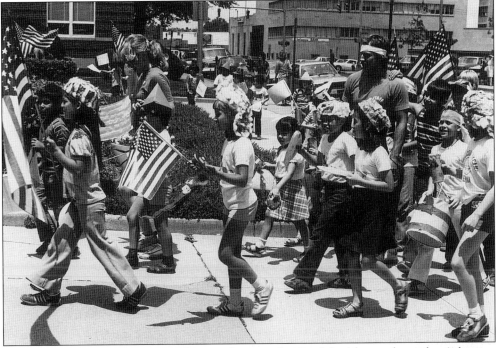

Children in patriotic dress wave flags as they march in a July 4th parade at the Arlington County Courthouse as a part of the county's annual parade. (ACPL/DE.)

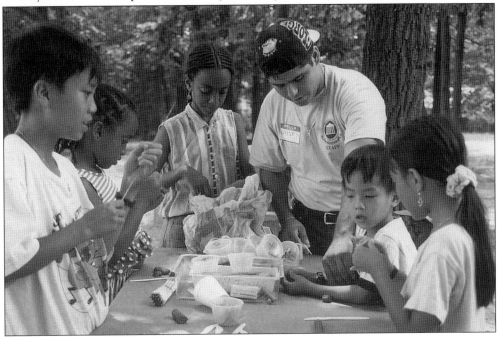

A staff member of the Arlington County Department of Parks, Recreation, and Community Resources assists children with crafts at a summer camp at Tyrol Hills Playground. These camps, held at many sites throughout the county, have become an important activity for children and their parents. (ACPL/DE.)

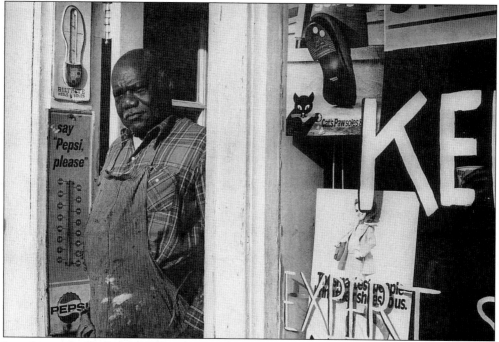

In a photo taken between 1979 and 1981, shoemaker Richard Walters is shown standing at the door of his shop in the Green Valley neighborhood of South Arlington. (ACPL/PD.)

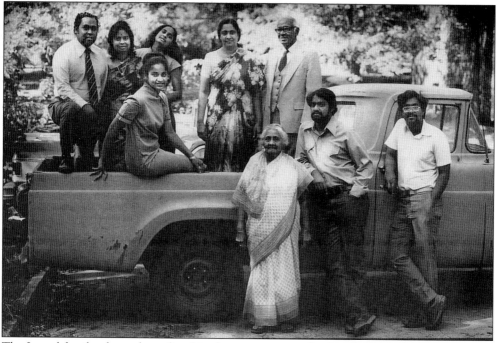

The Ismael family, shown here, lived in the apartments in Buckingham. In the last decades of the century, a number of recent immigrants made Buckingham their home. This photo was taken between 1979 and 1981. (ACPL/PD.)

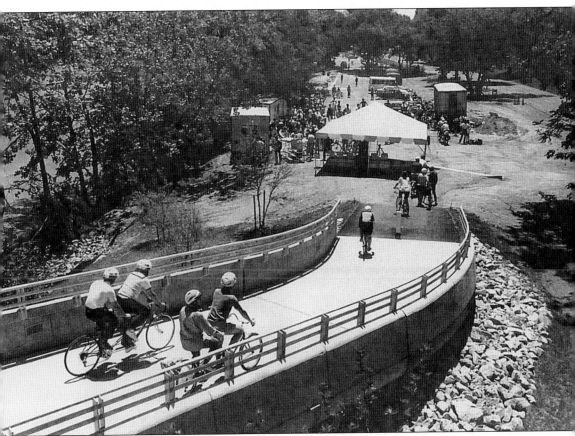

In 1988, a pedestrian and bicycle bridge was opened from Virginia's shore to Roosevelt Island. Called Analostan Island by early settlers, the island was later referred to as Barbadoes, or His Lordship's Island. When purchased by the third George Mason, it became Mason's Island. In 1931 the Roosevelt Memorial Association bought it to establish a national park in memory of conservation-minded President Theodore Roosevelt. (ACPL.)

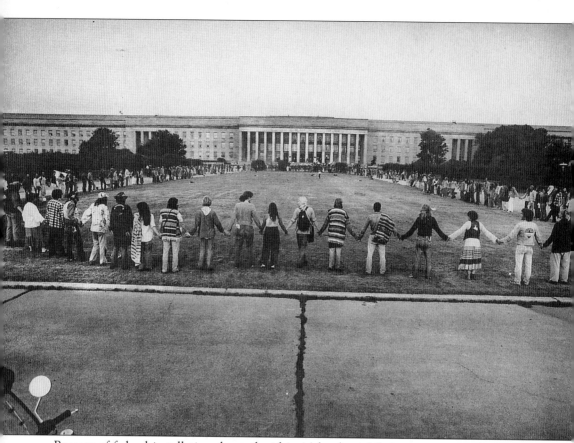

Because of federal installations located within its borders, Arlington sometimes becomes the locus of national events. Beginning in the late 1960s, the Pentagon was the site of large protests against American involvement in Vietnam. After the end of that conflict, smaller groups of demonstrators occasionally have converged there to protest U.S. military policy. Among these was the Rainbow Family demonstration on July 9, 1980, shown here at the Pentagon's River Entrance. (ACPL/PD.)